How You Can Beat Inflation

How You Can Beat Inflation

DAVID L. MARKSTEIN

McGRAW-HILL BOOK COMPANY

New York   St. Louis   San Francisco   Düsseldorf   London
Mexico   Panama   Sydney   Toronto

332
Ma /

Sponsoring Editors   M. Joseph Dooher/Dale L. Dutton
Director of Production   Stephen J. Boldish
Editing Supervisor   Carolyn Nagy
Editing and Production Staff   Gretlyn Blau,
   Teresa F. Leaden, George E. Oechsner

HOW YOU CAN BEAT INFLATION

Library of Congress Catalog Card Number: 71–134600

07–040427–5

1234567890   VBVB   7543210

To Yvette

Preface

"From the fury of the Northmen, Lord, deliver us!"

So PRAYED many of the inhabitants of Western Europe a thousand years ago. Their coasts were open to endless raids by the Vikings from Denmark, Norway, and Sweden. The French, English, Irish, Germans, and Spaniards underwent spasms of terror at news that long-ship crews had landed to harry and bedevil their lands, burn their homes, enslave their women, destroy their crops, and kill their cattle, along with whatever fighting men dared gather in scattered bands to oppose the Norse fury.

Today, a new fury is loose upon the land. It affects Northmen, along with populations of the South, the East, and the West. It has a name as fear-filling as that of the Vikings:

Inflation

It is fortunate that you do not have to lie down and die as inflation rolls over the land, as so many fear-filled Europeans of the Vikings' day lay down and died in paralyzed terror when the Northmen's ships were sighted standing toward land. You can do something about it. You can (1) try to build up your capital and your income faster than inflation erodes away their dwindling value; (2) organize to at least mitigate, and perhaps beat or halt, inflation both in your home and your home community.

The book goes into *how*.

Although I have written with the inflation of United States and Canadian dollars in mind and suggest steps that are workable in the North American economies and under North American democratic political systems, the problem is not ours alone. Inflation rages through the Western European lands where once the Northmen burned and pillaged the homes of honest inhabitants.

Common Market prices in 1969 increased 5.5 percent, according to official figures. That stacks against 4.5 percent the year earlier, and both the scope and degree of its increases are comparable to inflationary scope and acceleration in the United States. Even in Germany, once a bastion of solid currency and sound fiscal policies, inflation is burning and pillaging a sizable percentage of honest inhabitants' money.

At the time of the Northmen's raids, an effective combination of forces was often able to oppose and defeat the Vikings. Such combined and careful efforts today can oppose and, hopefully, mitigate the furious inflation that besets us all.

David L. Markstein

Contents

How You Can Beat Inflation

1

You Can Beat This Bogey!

"GOSH!" everyone says around October 12, when we celebrate Columbus Day in the U.S. "Isn't it a wonderful thing
that this man of vision sailed three little crackerbox Spanish
ships across an unknown sea and found the Americas!"

It does indeed seem a wonderful thing that Christopher
Columbus did. But for whom was it wonderful?

Certainly not for the people of Spain. That land, possessed
of but a primitive productive machine (as was all the civilized
world around the time the fifteenth century was turning into
the sixteenth), couldn't absorb the quantity of gold that eager
conquistadores were grabbing off in the New World and ship-
ping by the galleon to busy Spanish ports. The classic definition
of inflation calls for more money to chase the same goods. More
money did. Briefly prosperous, Spain soon sank—many serious
economic thinkers say it did so because of Columbus' wonder-

ful voyages of discovery—into poverty and became a European backwater in the later years that followed its first explosion of prosperity.

Even today, people don't complain about inflation until the time is pretty late in the progress of currency deterioration and, possibly, too late to stop the danged thing.

At first, as in Spain long ago, a little inflation brings about an illusion of great prosperity, much as a narcotic administered to ease the postoperative pain of a hospital patient produces euphoria along with the absence of hurt. Sober economists might warn that a little inflation is no more possible than a little pregnancy; inflation, like pregnancy, must grow. But people ignore warnings like that because they don't want anything to disturb the feeling of great happiness and joy that the inflationary narcotic brings.

Then things get a little less good.

As would be the case if doctors administered a great deal of pain-killing narcotic, the inflationary infusions of new money bring about a smaller and smaller growth of the happiness called "good times." Soon it takes a gigantic dose to make the patient feel that he is still progressing. And, again as would be the case in an overnarcoticized patient, the "good" medicine begins to bring about a deterioration of the body. In the case of inflation, it is the economic body which deteriorates. With both the human and the economic patient, the deterioration gets faster. The relief possible from inflationary dope becomes smaller. The dope itself becomes a disease worse than the original ill which it was administered to ease. *Now* the patient, whether an individual or a nation, at last realizes that he is hooked on something pretty bad and nearly impossible to throw off.

Many people think inflation is a new thing that has just come about in the last few years in the U.S. It is not. It grew to proportions where its inherent evil could be recognized because of massive infusions recently given to it. But the first doses began many years ago. Lots of us at first thought of them as "prosperity" or "boom times." The causes are long; the pay-off is now.

This book won't stop inflation. Not even if millions of copies were erected as a wall in the hope of keeping ravaging inflation outside. It might—if read in high places by the right people— give pause to those who are administering causative doses of money into the economy. *But, most important, it will, I hope, help* YOU *to beat the habit, to advance your income and increase your capital resources at a rate faster than inflation eats off their purchasing power.*

As a people, we may or we may not beat the inflationary menace. But as a person, you can beat it. This book will tell you how.

Inflation has been likened to a rat gnawing at a piece of cheese. The rat takes a little bite here and another little bite there. Eventually, he eats the cheese away. It may take him some time to do it. But suppose that the rat grows to the size of a horse. This giant-sized rat gobbles the whole cheese pretty quickly.

Something akin to that is happening. The cheese is vanishing in gobs and great chunks. To use the first simile again, the drug is taking over, and bigger and bigger doses of it are producing more and more deterioration in our ability to enjoy the good life. Before going into the things you can do as an individual to help run off the horse-sized rat, to take your body off the debilitating inflationary drug, consider some *logical* results to expect in ten years if (as it likely will) inflation continues:

Many scholars like to use the word "extrapolate." It has a pleasant, learned, polysyllabic sound. Roughly, it means to project. We will extrapolate from some conservative figures issued by the Bureau of Labor Statistics in Washington and see how far inflation at present rates of increase might carry us. I stress that this is conservative figuring because the BLS's statistics, while meticulously gathered and compiled, do not take into account the biggest part of inflationary price increases. They leave out a sizable part of the service industries. They fail to account for the $5.00 plumber's call that you could have had a decade ago, which now costs $15.00 and upward. They are not set up to be aware of the $3.00 bill for an office visit to a doctor, now grown into anywhere from $10.00 to $25.00. They do not even notice the higher cost of a shoeshine, a car wash, or adjusting bent eyeglasses.

Before me as this is written is a BLS release which shows that from January 1967 to January 1969, the consumer price index for urban wage earners rose from 114.7 to 124.1. Ten years ago, using the same months (January 1957 compared with January 1959), the rise was from 99.7 to 102.2. In two years during the decade of the fifties, inflation, measured by the BLS Consumer Price Index, went up by 4.8 percent. *But in two comparable years of the decade of the sixties, it went up 8.2 percent.*

Inflation is indeed picking up its rate of increase.

Consider where extrapolation of these basically conservative cost-of-living figures might carry us in another ten years.

An assumption is necessary before anyone can project figures or trends because none of us possesses a crystal ball or a mess of tea leaves capable of infallibly foretelling future events. Our assumption—and I repeat that it is, in my opinion, a very conservative one—will say that inflation won't abate. It might accelerate its pace still further in the next ten years. Acceleration of inflation, automobiles, snowslides, and other such things usually picks up ever faster until a point of terminal velocity is reached. In the case of a nation exposed to inflation, that point frequently coincides with national bankruptcy. But our assumption won't call for such ever-faster terminal rates of increase. We will say that the rate doubles in the next ten years as it did in the last decade. The assumption further says that the rate of every two years' increase will stay at 8.2 percent for the next four years. For the four years that follow them, it will be at 1.5 times that rate (12.3 percent), and for the final two-year period it will be at double the 1967–1969 rate.

That would raise the Consumer Price Index to a lofty 213.4.

At that level, the dollar would have depreciated in purchasing power by a further 72 percent.

Things look bad enough when you look at a bald figure like 72 percent. They look worse when you apply such a rate of inflation increase to the cost of some familiar things.

The medium-range car, presently priced, with accessories, in the area of $4,000.00, would then cost $6,880.00.

The $50.00 supermarket checkout ticket of today would have run up to $86.00 without your having purchased a single additional item.

The $35,000.00 home of today would be up in the area of $60,200.00 and not have a single air conditioner, kitchen fixture, or carpet added to it. If you now paid $200.00 per month to buy this house, ten years hence you would be writing a check in the amount of $344.00 every thirty days to pay your mortgage bill, if this assumption proves correct.

Staggering.

You would be in what today are considered upper-income cost brackets without necessarily having achieved upper-income frills and possibly without having achieved the upped kind of income necessary to merely stay even with inflation. (But don't fret yet. The purpose of this book is to put your income and your possessions up even faster than the dollar yardstick of value shrinks.)

If you think that my extrapolation of possible inflationary losses to come in the future is exaggerated, then read what one expert recently said. Writing in the October 1969 issue of *The Spectator*, Robert B. Johnson, Partner in Charge of Research for the big New York Stock Exchange house of Paine, Webber, Jackson and Curtis, noted:

> Yes, Virginia, there is something worse than inflation. And there is something worse than recession. What? Inflation and recession. Both. Simultaneously. You might say "the worst of both worlds." [Mr. Johnson outlined conditions now happening under which this unthinkable event might become reality.]

The powerful, 111-nation International Monetary Fund has been termed the central banker to all the world. In its 1969 annual report, the IMF noted that checking of inflation in Britain, the U.S., and France has been particularly difficult because of strong cost-push forces (more about these shortly). Hoping that late 1969 or 1970 would see significant changes in the inflationary fires of the American economy, IMF noted sadly that "failure of the U.S. economy to cool off must be rated as a major disappointment" of 1968. As 1969 was drawing to an end, the Fund must again have been disappointed, because no cooling off had become apparent. In fact, the inflationary heat is still very hot and "progress" of pay raises and price increases seems to be at a faster rate than ever.

So we begin with the premise that inflation in the future is nearly inevitable, despite probable temporary successes in damping it down, and that it will almost inevitably accelerate its rate of currency erosion, although there may be occasional years when prices will stand still or increase only minutely.

Your basic strategy for this situation is discussed in Chapter Two, which notes that heavy income taxation makes capital growth the only avenue in which gains can be achieved without being immediately confiscated. It tells how a small stake can get you started, and goes into ways to accumulate this if you do not already possess it, explores the logic of borrowing when the odds are that repayment will be made later in money of less value than money borrowed today, and looks over things on which you can make long-term loans and how to use others' funds by such gimmicks as leasing rather than buying many items. You'll see ways of turning income into capital and the mighty effect of plowback in accelerating capital growth.

Chapter Three examines the vast present size of institutions and how their hungry appetite for stocks almost guarantees a large—although not necessarily immediate or constant—growth in the prices of common stocks. It will tell you about the effective growth stock approach, with a report on research by the U.S. Department of Commerce on pace-setting industries. The chapter further differentiates true growth from seeming growth, shows how to spot when growth stocks stop growing, and explains the technique of speculation in whatever appears to be moving and how to grab such stocks before their big movements come. You will see how professionals bail out of the market when clouds gather and learn about the use of leverage to multiply money.

Chapter Four shows what mutual funds are. Go-go funds set out to beat the market and each other, but there is danger when a go-go fund stumbles. The chapter gives criteria for judging when to buy and when to sell and shows how to use insurance to have an accumulative fund plan paid up if you should die. Also detailed is the sophisticated 50-50 Fund Idea (mixing mutuals with swinging stocks).

In Chapter Five we'll consider how raw land has appreciated over the years, examples of land that remained stable in value while other areas soared (you'll want to avoid purchasing such land as a medieval villager would avoid the plague), ten questions to ask in judging the appreciation potential of land, whether you should add buildings, building only after leasing, the arithmetic of apartments, shopping centers, etc., and ways to leverage these using only moderate capital of your own.

Special opportunities in real estate are considered in Chapter Six. Examples are the building of post offices to be rented to the U.S. (a plan by which many people with small capital have leveraged their way to possession of a paid-up valuable asset in twenty years), the remodeling and reselling market for run-down real estate in good neighborhoods, country real estate in resort areas and how demand plus extra leisure almost guarantees a spurt in value for such scarce land over the years to come, building amusement areas to further capitalize on this demand (and doing so with small starting capital), and borrowing at low interest while lending at high interest.

Once the preserve of the wealthy, petroleum participations are within reach of us all today. The possibilities in these are examined in Chapter Seven, which shows what this new form of investment is, its tax advantages, and the enormous inflation hedge it offers. In such participations you might strike it very rich very suddenly, yet, through diversification now available to the smaller investor, you need risk far less than if you backed a wildcatter of oil exploration's older days. Some participations are more attractive than others, depending upon an investor's circumstances; this chapter looks into the factors that make them so and offers guidelines for choosing a petroleum play.

Chapter Eight's theme is a farm to fight inflation. It goes into the citrus grove bit and the capital gains it offers, how you can play this angle even if you don't know an orange from a grapefruit. Even those of us whose nearest contact with a cow is the shoot-'em-up Western seen on a TV late show can hedge against inflation with cattle on the hoof. Pros will sell you a herd, manage it, feed it, carry it to market, and sell it, freeing the city-feller investor—and even the small-towner who does know cattle but lacks time to manage them for himself—from worries and from many of the risks of cattle raising. The chapter also takes a look at the brand-new hedge of catfish farming.

In Chapter Nine you'll see how at times some commodities are better than money. Basic things human beings need nearly always go up faster than money goes down; copper, paladium, and platinum are examples. Even if you can't buy a copper mine or stockpile red metal by the ton, you can buy futures contracts. Chapter Nine explains what these are and the dangers inherent in their volatility (commodities must be seen from the short-term point of view because of the nature of the commodity contract). Other contents of Chapter Nine are: the things to look for in judging possibilities for a rise, use of the commodity trader's tool—charting, examples from the past, and a different kind of "future" commodity—called scotch whisky.

It helps to mind your business—this is the theme of Chapter Ten, which explores the possibilities in becoming a self-employed businessman with the potential to see his income grow faster than wages or salaries paid those on corporate payrolls. It shows both sideline and full-time possibilities. Although statistics indicate that an alarming percentage of new businesses go broke during their first and second years, this chapter shows you one kind of business operation in which the odds of making money—sometimes big money—are as much as ten times better than in run-of-the-mill small businesses. It shows what to look for if you buy a going concern and how to get it at a good price, and it warns of the pitfall signals which might mean that you are paying a high price for a business already skidding into bankruptcy. There are important sources of financial and how-to-do-it operating help for small businessmen, and you will learn what these are in Chapter Ten.

Chapter Eleven takes a different theme. It shows ways to make inflation-threatened dollars at least partly secure from the inflationary rat's nibbling by making them buy more even at a time when over-all puchasing power for people who are less well informed than you is eroding badly. A number of specific ideas will be discussed for making the same money stay longer in your bank account and buy more value in specific big-ticket purchases such as a family automobile. It tells how to make, then how to live within, a family budget.

Ways to combine with your neighbors for presenting a group front opposed to the causes of inflation are discussed in Chapter Twelve, which tells how to mobilize Neighborhood Power.

But you can do all things wisely, yet lose the purchasing power of your income at the end. Most retirement planning is angled toward finding good hobbies or moving to places where retiree neighbors will have the same interests and needs as your own. Chapter Thirteen's bag is how to avoid the plight of the fellow who saved all of his life, yet found himself unable to enjoy good things of the retirement years because his planning had been on a scale where $75.00 per month rented a retirement cottage and $2.00 bought a steak dinner, with the morning newspaper available for a nickel.

The fact is—inflation is *not* an unbeatable thing. There have been some terrifying inflations in the past in other nations. Yet out of these, shrewd, far-sighted people who recognized the situation and, instead of weeping or wringing their hands, took steps to fight it on a personal basis, emerged unscathed and in some instances better off than before the inflation started.

France at the time of the Revolution was menaced on its borders by monarchist nations determined to crush the upstart experiment in Continental democracy. The Revolutionary authorities decreed the raising of armies to fight on all of France's borders simultaneously—and quickly found that armies need more than manpower—that they also need money for weapons, supplies, food, clothing, and transportation. Bankrupt France had little of the "hard" money of the time, which consisted of gold and silver. "No sweat," said the financially unsophisticated leaders of the time. "We will pay for everything with paper money. When we have won our wars and the nation is back on its feet, we will redeem the paper money with gold and silver wrung from our enemies." They called this issue of paper *assignats.*

Soon, the inevitable happened. Weapons makers, suppliers, clothing manufacturers, even the soldiers themselves, were reluctant to accept assignats. Every day a bundle of assignats bought less. Inflation set in.

Throughout the troubled assignat period, people who were smart noticed that others were being forced to sell jewels, real goods, land, anything, to keep up their ability to continue buying bread with ever-diminishing assignats. These smarter folk, instead of selling, used their assignats to buy, and out of the troubles of the times and the miseries of inflation emerged a new class of rich folk—those who had employed legal currency to obtain things better than money, possessed of a value which lasted until stability was restored. True, some were despised as profiteers and most of us would consider them so today. But they survived, and that was no mean feat in Revolutionary France.

Defeated Germany at the end of World War I lay prostrate and began printing marks on its presses with such abandon that it was said no one knew how high he had to load his wheelbarrow—if he still had one—with paper marks in order to bring home a loaf of bread from the grocery. Prices would go up every day. Then twice a day. Finally, many times daily. There is a thick sheaf of paper still nestling in my bank box. It consists of mark bonds issued at that time, the investment of a relative, now dead, who believed—looking from his vantage point in New York—that financially prostrate Germany would rise again and that German bonds would be redeemed. They are presently worth less than the paper on which they are printed, for the mark of the Weimar Republic was never made good. It vanished. With it went the savings of all who had not the necessary wit to desert the mark and buy whatever lasting goods could be obtained for the dwindling German money.

Much nearer to us in time and distance is the case of Chile.

The official rate of inflation there was running between 25 percent and 35 percent *a year* in the late 1960s. In an article on this terrifying inflation, "Inflation, Latin Style," the *Wall Street Journal,* in its issue of August 6, 1969, reported the comment of a Chilean engineer caught in an inevitable squeeze between rising costs and slower-rising income. "To save money in Chile, you have to buy things as fast as you can," it quoted twenty-nine-year-old Patricio Grunberg, a construction engineer in the city of Santiago, as saying.

Señor Grunberg had put his finger on the way to survive an inflation: *Buy things.*

"Things" at the time of the French Revolution consisted of jewels, furniture, palaces, and farm lands. Some things were productive, such as farm lands. Some were useful, such as living quarters. Some had intrinsic value because of rarity, acceptance, and workmanship, such as jewels. Things were worth more than assignats, and the savvy *citoyens* of the time swapped worthless paper money for objects useful in themselves or functional as storehouses of value.

"Things" in Germany of the 1920s were more sophisticated. Smart Germans did not invest, as did my late uncle, in bonds worth a set number of marks. They instead bought productive capacity in plants. They bought stocks, most of which ended up better havens of capital than either the weak Weimar government or that government's money. They purchased commodities. They looked for things which would be worth as much in real purchasing value later on and which might, with luck and given good judgment and good fortune, appreciate in value vis-à-vis purchasing power.

"Things" in Señor Grunberg's Chile of today—a nation not as financially or industrially advanced as Germany or the United States and Canada—consist of Volkswagens, jewelry, Swiss bank deposits, and, by no means last, with knowledgeable Chileans, investments in U.S. stocks, mutual funds, and the like.

There, reiterated, is the lesson of how smart people survive: they move from money to things.

But, as we have seen, the things which successfully survive

and function as storehouses of value are not the same in every place or at every time of inflation. I do not believe for a moment that we in the United States face anything as disastrous as the German inflation of the twenties, or that our money will ever become quite as worthless as Revolutionary France's assignats. Nor do I think inflation will mount to such a pace here as Chile's 25 percent to 35 percent a year (although that is possible unless the inflationary fires are contained).

Still, such inflation as we have and as threatens to accelerate in the future can make you a lot poorer. Our purpose is to study the kinds of things best calculated to get you out on the other side of the North American inflation unscarred and, if possible, richer than you are today in realistic terms of the products and services with which you can grace your life.

Consider what has already happened here:

■ The Bureau of Labor Statistics' figures show that over-all food costs have soared over 25 percent in a decade. Expressed in terms of 1957–1959 dollars, food which once cost $1.00 at the checkout counter would run, on average, about $1.25 as this is written. The rate of increase, however, is increasing. Since a year previous, BLS reported in 1969, it soared 5.4 percent. Eating out in a restaurant has soared even more. The statistics —which most of us who find dinner and luncheon checks a lot higher would dispute—show an increase of 43.7 percent in the decade and 5.9 percent since last year.

■ Your 1959 house which cost $10,000.00 ran, on average, $12,600 in 1969. Few home buyers would agree with this figure, saying that costs have risen considerably more than that. The 1968 to 1969 rise, BLS said, was 6.4 percent on average.

■ Apparel and upkeep, the Bureau stated, run $1.27 for every $1.00 you spent ten years back, and increased by 5.9 percent in the past twelve months alone. If you were to read a newspaper of ten years ago, however, it would appear that the rate must have been higher, for $100.00 men's suits of that time are in the $175.00 bracket now, and the $4.00 to $5.00 men's shirt is now an $8.95 item. A dress costing $50.00 would be almost $100.00 now.

■ Medical care has had one of the greatest increases. The

doctor who sent you a bill for $1.00 in 1959 now charges $1.55, assuming any doctor every charged either of these moderate figures. Medical and health care costs are up 7.5 percent in the last year alone. From my own experience, a private hospital room costing $34.00 per day in 1965 ran $100.00 per day in 1969—and the service was slower and the harried nurses fewer.

In each of the instances above, the rate of decrease in the dollar's purchasing power had increased alarmingly in the previous twelve months. That is the terrifying thing about current inflation. The New York State Department of Agriculture and Markets reported on changes in New York City retail prices of selected meat cuts from July 1968 to July 1969. It showed that porterhouse steak was up, on average, from $1.39 to $1.49 per pound—a 7.2 percent price jump—and sirloin, from $1.19 to $1.39—up 16.8 percent; that chuck steak had risen from 64 cents to 79 cents, or 23.4 percent. Turkey, costing 47 cents per pound in 1968, tended to be sold at 52 cents in 1969, a seemingly tiny increase of 5 cents, which nevertheless represented a hike of 10.6 percent. Veal loin chops, running at $1.44 one year previous, rose to $1.74, up 20.8 percent. In all, twenty cuts were listed, and *all of them were up.*

No housewife needs to be told that the whole supermarket checkout ticket has increased along with the cost of meat and frequently in excess of the meat cost increases found in New York City in July 1969. "I have to buy for two fewer people than I fed five years ago, yet I cash a check twice as big when I shop the supermarket," a friend told me. Her experience, other women say, is typical.

It is true that wages and salaries tend to go up as well as prices. Often, however, they go up after price increases. Most of us run faster all of the time in the hope of staying in the same place. If the inflationary treadmill steps up its pace, we may soon drop behind (see Table 1 and Figure 1).

How did our world fall apart so quickly? What has made such inflationary things happen to our once powerful and stable currency? An understanding of causes will be helpful in the application of the personal cures to be explored in later chapters.

TABLE 1

	Indexes of value of money (1958 = 100)		Annual rates of depreciation		
	1963	1968	'58–'68*	'66–'67	'67–'68
Guatemala	100	98	0.2%	0.5%	1.9%
El Salvador	102	97	0.3	1.4	2.5
Venezuela	95	92	0.9	− 1.0	1.0
Thailand	101	89	1.2	3.8	2.2
United States	94	83	1.9	2.7	4.0
Greece	92	83	1.9	1.6	0.4
Honduras	95	83	1.9	2.5	2.2
Luxembourg	95	82	2.0	2.2	2.5
Canada	94	81	2.2	3.5	3.9
South Africa	93	80	2.2	3.3	1.8
Germany (Fed. Rep.)	90	80	2.2	1.7	1.6
Australia	92	79	2.2	3.1	2.6
Belgium	94	79	2.3	2.8	2.7
Morocco	83	79	2.3	− 0.8	0.5
Mexico	90	77	2.5	2.9	2.2
Switzerland	90	76	2.7	3.8	2.3
Jamaica	85	75	2.8	2.8	3.7
Pakistan	94	74	2.9	6.5	0.2
United Kingdom	90	74	2.9	2.4	4.5
New Zealand	90	74	3.0	5.7	4.1
Austria	87	73	3.0	3.8	2.7
Iran	79	73	3.1	1.6	0.7
Ireland	91	73	3.1	3.0	4.6
Netherlands	90	72	3.2	3.3	3.6
Italy	86	72	3.2	3.1	1.4
Portugal	90	72	3.3	5.2	5.7
Norway	88	72	3.3	4.2	3.4
Ecuador	87	72	3.3	2.2	4.7
Sweden	87	70	3.5	4.1	1.9
France	80	69	3.8	2.6	4.4
Philippines	86	68	3.8	5.7	− 0.1
Finland	86	62	4.7	5.4	7.7
Japan	79	62	4.7	3.8	5.1
Israel	78	61	4.9	1.6	2.1
Denmark	82	60	4.9	7.7	7.1
China (Taiwan)	68	60	5.0	3.2	7.3

TABLE 1 (Continued)

	Indexes of value of money (1958 = 100)		Annual rates of depreciation		
	1963	1968	'58–'68*	'66–'67	'67–'68
Spain	78	54	5.9	6.1	4.7
India	87	54	5.9	11.7	3.1
Bolivia	66	48	7.1	7.1	4.9
Turkey	65	47	7.3	12.8	5.6
Iceland	74	44	7.8	3.2	12.0
Colombia	61	37	9.6	7.6	5.5
Peru	68	37	9.6	8.7	16.2
Yugoslavia	71	34	10.2	6.5	6.2
Korea	64	32	10.8	9.8	9.7
South Vietnam	84	23	13.5	30.4	22.0
Chile	37	11	20.1	15.3	21.0
Argentina	20	7	23.8	22.7	13.9
Brazil	15	2	32.1	22.8	19.5
Indonesia	8	†	58.9	62.9	55.6

* Compounded annually.   † Less than one.

NOTE: Depreciation computed from unrounded data. Value of money is measured by reciprocals of official cost-of-living or consumer price indexes.
SOURCE: First National City Bank of New York, *Monthly Economic Letter,* July, 1969.

Let us go back to that classic cause of inflation we met in Spain of the post-Columbus years: More money chasing the same amount of goods. Inflations begin that way. Our present inflation, sometimes quiescent and sometimes raging but always present, began that way. It may have come now to a point where, no longer needing the monetary cause, it feeds upon itself; we will examine that possibility shortly. But the first cause was an increase in money. To grasp how this happened, we have to look at what our money is and how it comes to exist. Long ago, money was stuff that had been coined out of gold or silver. But gold is not used in our coinage, and its possession, except for jewelry and collectors' items, is not even legal for U.S. citizens. Silver vanished as a monetary metal during the mid-1960s. Our paper money is no longer redeemable in either precious metal.

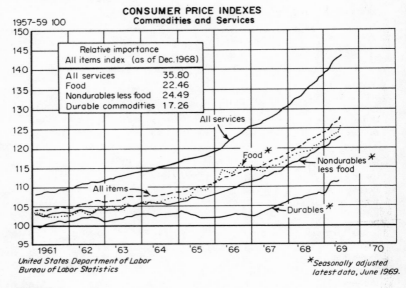

CONSUMER PRICE INDEXES
Commodities and Services

1957-59 100

Relative importance	
All items index (as of Dec.1968)	
All services	35.80
Food	22.46
Nondurables less food	24.49
Durable commodities	17.26

United States Department of Labor
Bureau of Labor Statistics

*Seasonally adjusted
latest data, June 1969.

FIGURE 1

Shells have functioned as money at times in man's history. So have war clubs. In certain societies in certain eras, prices have been quoted in hides, cattle, and donkeys. Our money is none of those things.

In fact, it is hard to say what money is, as we use it today. The best description is that our money is a *concept*. It is money because we say it is. As long as we say this, it will be able to buy things. If the monetary authorities inflate it by making more of it than our productivity increases can absorb, the more money chases fewer goods, just as it did in Spain, in France, in Germany, and in Chile. Yet, as long as the concept remains rooted, the stuff we use is still money. If inflations proceed far enough, the concept is no longer accepted. Then we have the national debacles and personal catastrophes which befell other inflation-ridden countries at other times and places.

Examine the "making" of money:

■ When banks grew, they began lending out part of the gold and silver deposits people left with them. Then, when there were one million florins or ducats on deposit, and the bank lent against 750,000 of the coinage—keeping the actual currency but giving instead a credit memo showing that the borrower had the appropriate ducats and florins with which he could purchase—the bank had graduated to creating money. It took one million florins and turned them at the swish of a feather quill pen into 1,750,000—a neat trick and potentially inflationary, unless there were enough new goods to mop up the newly created purchasing power.

■ Later, central banks had to be instituted to control this process, since the bankers from time to time took off on sprees of creativity that ended with the depositors queued up for money and panic gripping the nation.

■ Now central banks do the money creation trick. In fact, central banks control the money completely. Central bankers like to deny this. But in the November 1969 *Review* of the Federal Reserve Bank of St. Louis, Michael W. Keran of the Research Department of the St. Louis Federal Reserve Bank noted: "This article . . . presents evidence that the movements of the money stock have been dominated by the behavior of the monetary authorities and not by the behavior of the public."

Darryl R. Francis, President of the same Federal Reserve Bank, noted this fact in greater detail in a speech he made May 12, 1969, before a convention of the Arkansas Bankers Association:

> The Federal Reserve System, through its power to create and destroy bank reserves, can control the money supply. Since there are close causal links between changes in Federal Reserve actions and in the money supply and between changes in the money supply and changes in spending, I submit that the money supply gives us the best overall measure of the influence of monetary policy actions.
>
> An example of the difference between the use of interest rates and the growth of money as indicators of the thrust of monetary actions is found in early 1968. Throughout the first half of 1968 the Federal Open Market Committee agreed that a restrictive monetary policy was appropriate. However, at several of the

Committee meetings, the proceedings of which has been published, some participants argued that a substantial degree of monetary restraint had already been achieved, as indicated by the high and rising market interest rates. Now it is true that interest rates rose rapidly through the first five months of last year, but these rising prices of funds were the result of very strong demands for credit enlarged by the anticipation that inflation would be with us for quite a while longer. If the rising interest rates a year ago indicated "a substantial degree of monetary restraint," then when will this economy feel the effects of that restraint?

In contrast to the unreliable signposts provided by interest rates, the money stock indicator pointed in the direction that the economy actually moved. The money stock grew at a very rapid 7 per cent annual rate in the first half of last year, about as rapid as in any six-month period in the past twenty years. This rapid monetary growth in early 1968 has since been stimulating the economy. It was not surprising to those who observe the economy from the monetary point of view that there was little slowing in total spending in late 1968 and early 1969, *and no improvement in the inflation problem* [italics mine].

There are many ways in which monetary authorities expand or contract our money supply. They can do this through "open market" activities based upon purchases and sales of government bonds. (A simplified example: The Fed decides to pump another $10 billion into the economy. It buys $10 billion in Treasury bonds in the open market. These are purchased from a dealer named Bill Bondman. To pay for the bonds, the Fed credits the account of the bank in which Bondman and Company maintains its account. The bank, in turn, applies $10 billion credit to Bondman and Company's account. Suddenly, there is a $10 billion credit in the economy which, before this action, did not exist.)

The Fed also exercises control over money growth and contraction by governing the amount of reserves which banks must maintain. (Simplified example: The Gotwads National Bank has deposits of $5 billion. It must maintain reserves of $1 billion, or 20 percent. If the Federal Reserve changes that requirement to permit retention of only 15 percent reserves, the

Gotwads National suddenly has $500 million which it can lend, and those lent dollars flood out through the economy. They are an *increase*. They may have existed before the change, but they did not have the capacity to make purchases before people borrowed the freed $500 million from Gotwads.

In 1969, anxious to cool off inflation and convinced that a tightening of money with an increase in interest rates would bring off the job, the Fed clamped a ceiling on Regulation Q. This regulation sets the top interest rate which banks are allowed to pay for money they borrow. Unable to borrow additional funds to lend out, the banks' activities tended to slow. (However, some smart bankers found ways around this dilemma. The Regulation Q control is cited here for its potential to slow money growth and for its ability to become an engine of inflation if handled in reverse of the way Federal Reserve planners applied it in 1969.)

By these and other means, the central bank has become the father of our money. No longer do banks merely hold it in safekeeping. Led by the top bank of all, the Fed, they make and withdraw the stuff.

Thus money is a concept. It is whatever the authorities say it is, *and it remains so as long as the people believe the financial authorities.*

Trouble comes when their belief turns to skepticism. They ask bigger prices for the things they sell and higher wages and salaries for their work, because they no longer believe in the "concept" of a dollar that is offered to them. They see that the dollar is not a constant.

Inflation!

But the Fed's actions alone are not to blame for the inflation which so sorely beset the U.S. in the waning years of the sixties. Inflation is something which soon feeds on itself. It becomes its own cause.

For example, there is "cost-push" inflation, which was mentioned earlier. In a classic study on inflation's causes ("Henry VIII Revisited"), the *Business Review* of the Federal Reserve Bank of Philadelphia wrote:

The cost-push theory of inflation rests on the premise that fundamental changes have taken place in our economy during the twentieth century. The theory points out that business firms have expanded in size and influence. Labor unions have grown in strength and bargaining power. Indeed, according to the cost-push thesis, labor today is so powerful at the bargaining table that it can push up wages faster than productivity (output per man-hour). Consequently, costs per unit of output increase. And rising costs are a source of great concern to management.

As costs rise, management has two choices. It can absorb the increased cost and thus experience falling profit margins; or it can pass costs on to the consumer in the form of higher prices if in a market position to do so. Since business has grown in influence and market power, there is a tendency to choose the latter alternative—to raise prices rather than lose profits.

But what does this have to do with money and the State? Plenty, say the cost-push theorists.

In 1946, Congress passed a law—the Employment Act of 1946 —which, among other things, calls upon the Federal Government to help maintain maximum employment. To achieve this objective, it is necessary for virtually all goods produced to be purchased, even at higher price levels generated by cost-push pressures. If some goods are not bought business will lay off workers. There will be unemployment.

But where will we get the additional money to purchase the same amount of goods at higher prices? Not every salary of every worker will be raised.

For a time, we shall be able to draw down our cash balances and savings accounts. But there is a limit to the extent people will spend their hard-earned savings and part with cash. At this point they will decrease their consumption. Then, conclude the cost-push theorists, the Federal Government is forced to step in. To maintain employment, the State must take steps to increase the amount of money available for spending. In short, it would be forced to *manufacture money*.

The first cause of the inflation of the late sixties was such money manufacture. Three years earlier I had been asked a question by my older daughter, then a high school senior: "What does this talk of a $20 billion federal deficit mean—to me?" She was told: "It probably means prices 30 percent to 50 percent higher for everything you buy three years hence, since this should force the Federal Reserve to expand the money supply."

If you look at most 1966 prices compared with those of 1969, the prediction came about. For to meet that $20 billion deficit, money had to be manufactured. The concept of money was stretched a little.

But while the sudden, rapid expansion of the money supply brought about conditions for almost terrifying price increases in the same way that the conquistadores' gold imports into sixteenth-century Spain brought about conditions for higher prices in that country at that time, the inflation here—as happens with inflations—soon began to fatten without outside cause. Cost-push set in. Each price increase tended to trigger a wage increase demand. Everybody got into the act. Manufacturers, merchants, sellers of services, and professional people wanted higher prices and fees so they could keep up with whoever their private Joneses happened to be. The unions wanted increased wages so their members could pay the higher prices of goods. The sellers of manufactured goods required higher prices because their wage costs had gone up. Even Congress and the administration, outwardly dedicated to opposing inflation, contributed to its continuance when, in December 1969, Social Security benefits were raised.

Whose fault was all of this?

While it began with the Fed's need to finance the whopping deficits of a few years earlier, by the time 1969 rolled around everybody who contributed to inflation and who pushed the inflationary snowball downhill ever faster almost *had* to do what he did. It was that or lose out. Nobody was a villain. Inflation itself had become the villain. It had acquired a life and a will of its own.

Thus the inflation which at first had monetary causes grew a different set of causes. Today's inflation becomes the father of tomorrow's increased inflation, which in its turn begets a still greater inflation to come.

There is a final potential cause. It could—although it probably won't—bring about almost total inflation. The actions of foreign governments in supporting or devaluing their currencies and in furthering national economic interests affect our money.

The U.S. dollar is a mainstay of international trade. Most of this trade is based upon, if not always carried out in, United States money. From time to time, economically weaker countries have devalued their currencies in an effort to bolster sagging trade balances. (Simplified example: British wages rise, so that British goods cost more if sold in the U.S. than they formerly did. British foreign sales suffer as a result. What to do? The British government devalues the pound sterling, say by 10 percent. Now each American dollar possessed by a stateside consumer interested in purchasing British manufactures will buy a correspondingly greater amount of British goods, and the English import suddenly again becomes competitive with other merchandise on American store shelves.)

If sudden, sizable devaluations occur in important foreign currencies, the American dollar can be dragged down, because we are not immune to the competitive necessities of life which motivate economic planners of other lands.

Why isn't something being done about all of this?

Throughout the troubled year of 1969, the Nixon administration grappled with inflation. The Federal Reserve came to its assistance. Yet, despite the size, power, and prestige of these two mighty forces, inflation seemed to flip aside their best efforts as easily as a judo black belt would shrug off the efforts of a pair of untrained opponents.

Tight money was tried. In 1969, funds became awesomely expensive. Not within memory of man in the United States did interest rates rise so high. The federal government itself felt the pinch—yet President Nixon and his allies in the Fed pushed on their efforts. The Treasury had to pay 7.7 percent in December to get three-month money through Treasury bills. The best-known bulwark of corporate conservatism in the country, American Telephone and Telegraph, old Mother Bell herself, had to pay 9.1 percent on a long-term bond issue of one of her subsidiaries. Construction money cost 9 percent and more, if you could find it. Some borrowers counted themselves lucky to get money at 12 percent. Usury became usual.

That should have slowed inflation. It should have stopped a great deal of the overheated economic activity in the U.S. and so have contributed to a stabilization of prices by making it unprofitable for money to chase goods so ardently.

But it didn't.

At the same time that it became more expensive, money became scarcer. The growth in the money supply came to a halt. Since the normal needs of the economic animal tend to increase as his size increases, measured (among other ways) by the number of the population which feed upon him, a slight increase in the money supply becomes necessary for normal economic growth. That increase went by the boards. There was, by midsummer of 1969, no increase in the money supply.

"That," thought many of the planners, "should slow inflation."

But it did not stop inflation. Inflationary price increases continued. Great worry was expressed over the possibility that things had been carried too far and unwanted deflation (instead of stabilization) might result. Yet in December a number of industries announced price increases. These increases at the manufacturer's level grew in percentage size as they filtered down to the consumer level.

example You raise prices of baseball bats by 10 percent. The wholesaler, finding costs up 10 percent and his margin shriveling, adds his normal markup percentage not only to the new price but to the price increase, then figures in a few extra nickels—and lo! the bats cost 20 percent more when they reach the retailer. He, too, adds markup to the increase and pads on an extra few cents to make the retail price come out to a more even figure. The bats now cost 30 percent extra in the stores.

Officials also tried to make it harder to increase capital expenditures in the form of new plant construction and new equipment for factories. "Are they crazy?" asked one economist in wonder. "The only thing likely to keep productivity apace with labor increases is better equipment for labor to use. They are stopping that inflation-fighting force instead of stopping inflation."

The economist was wrong. Governmental efforts did not stop that inflation-fighting force (nor did they stop inflation), for capital spending continued to be a factor in the economy as manufacturers worried that even if new plant and equipment cost more with high interest and inflation, it would cost still more not to have it. A survey late in the year showed expectation of an 11 percent increase in 1970 capital output.

Banks' ability to lend was severely curtailed by the clamp on Regulation Q. But, unable to borrow domestically because people were putting savings into higher-yielding areas than bank savings accounts, the banks found new ways to borrow money. One of these was through repatriation of Eurodollars. Until the Fed made that harder to do, the ceiling on Regulation Q failed to halt bank lending.

Or inflation.

Jawboning was tried. Central-bank speakers figuratively shook their fists at the economy and announced their determination to hold to their restrictive courses come recession, unemployment, or whatever. The President made speeches to explain what he was trying to do and to ask cooperation of the business community, labor unions, and other groups capable of making cost-push inflation continue.

But cost-push inflation continued.

A group of industrialists tried the jawboning tactic, urging the construction contractors with whom many of them dealt to hold costs down and particularly to resist pressure for inflationary wage increases asked by their workers.

"They must think I'm nuts," one contractor told me at the time. "Resist, and I am out of business. I have to survive, and so, rightly or wrongly, I have to go along with most of the package asked of me. Besides—on cost-plus contracts I'm not losing anything."

And so jawboning by the august leaders of industry fared about as well as the jawboning of political and monetary leaders. Construction costs went up, triggering higher costs (and hence price increases) in other industries. Inflation laughed at jawboning.

Yet classic steps can bring at least a slowdown to inflation. The question is: Even if effective in the near future, and if at the time you read this book inflation appears to have been effectively quietened—*how long will non-inflation last?*

Can we hold to price stability?

Many serious thinkers believe that, given the welfare state and a world-wide willingness in all nations to face anything except hardship, *there may be no permanent cure for inflation.*

Let's repeat that.

There may be no permanent cure for inflation.

Not in this complicated, welfare-minded, austerity-hating world of people who have enjoyed a generation of complete ease and increasing prosperity. People have come to believe that more leisure with less work, and abolition of need from the earth, are achievable goals. It is not the purpose of this book to consider whether that aim is right or wrong, achievable or not. The effort to achieve it is almost certain to bring about a new breakout of inflation even if the present rounds of it are stopped.

"Sure," say some thinkers, "cost-push is not an easy force to stop. Not as easy as the direct monetary cause of inflation. But we can bottle up its effects at the source with wage and price controls." Both of these controls, alas, have been tried and have failed. The ancient Babylonian kings and the Egyptian pharaohs attempted price-wage controls; the emperors of long-ago Rome tried them. And the economic activity of Babylon, Egypt, and the Roman Empire stagnated.

Price and wage controls tend to turn men's energies and assets into channels which are not controlled. Rents covered by a ceiling? So we'll invest in stocks. Next, nobody tends the real estate store and soon properties deteriorate; owners cannot afford to fix them up at fixed prices. Good quarters grow scarce. It works that way with buildings, butter, neckties, automobiles, or buttonhooks. Clamp on a price lid and suddenly—no merchandise at any price.

Writing in the November 1969 *Monthly Review* of his bank,

Monroe Kimbrel, President of the Federal Reserve Bank of Atlanta, noted:

> As for myself, I am opposed to a system of direct wage and price controls because it runs contrary to my general philosophy and because I believe such a system would inevitably result in failure. Philosophically, I am opposed to direct controls because they would eliminate economic freedom. . . . Furthermore, I have not yet been shown where a system of direct controls has been an outstanding success. If you are looking for an example of the difficulties and distortions involved in direct controls, you have only to study experiences in this country during and after World War II. . . . Perhaps persons advocating direct controls naïvely believe that these controls will be selective and will pick on someone else instead of them. Perhaps businessmen hope that controls will be imposed on wages and on prices of things they buy but will not be on their profits and the things they sell. But you and I know that once started, there will be no limit to the facets of our economy which eventually will be placed under restrictions and controls.

Said Darryl R. Francis, President of the St. Louis Federal Reserve Bank: "Direct controls, like a new paint job over a termite-infested house, hide the evidence but do nothing to eliminate the cause of the problem."

As it has become increasingly apparent that inflation, whether temporarily stopped or not, is part of the American scene, two popular personal approaches to inflation beating have been tried—and failed. It is well to examine these lest we become swept up in popular enthusiasm for panaceas.

■ One was the purchase of gold stocks. Americans are forbidden by law to own gold, but they can legally own the common stocks of gold-mining corporations. If, runs the theory behind this ploy, the official price of gold should be raised from its present $35.00 per ounce, the profits of gold miners would have to soar, since all of the new money received from the sale of gold would go into net profit. Gold companies would, moreover, be able to bring into production mines which are presently unprofitable, since a higher price would justify using the lower-grade ores of these mines. Gold-mining stocks would have to soar.

A convincing argument.

Unfortunately, however, the price of gold has not gone up. Keeping that sacrosanct $35.00-per-ounce peg has become a fetish with American governments. A change in the price of gold seems to many to be like downgrading American motherhood or coming out flatfooted for sin. One doesn't do such things. The longer one doesn't, the more binding and authentic seems the fetish.

World trade is now lubricated by a new kind of "money" in place of gold. It is called "Special Drawing Rights" and is administered by the International Monetary Fund much as the Federal Reserve administers the dollar. SDR's are a kind of concept money, as the dollar, pound, franc (French, not Swiss), yen, peso, peseta, mark, and even the ruble are concept currencies. The rational-concept moneys represent ability to buy goods. The Special Drawing Rights represent settlement wampum for handling purchases and sales of goods between nations.

Therefore gold has proved no protection. Gold-mining stocks —unless bought quickly at the start of a cyclical upswing triggered by gold price-increase rumors and sold quickly when the upswing tops because of the death of the rumor—haven't proved a hedge against anything except riches.

■ Assets in the ground have long bemused certain inflation thinkers. Their theory is that as long as usable assets, such as petroleum, copper, and iron, stay in the ground, these hedge against future inflation. When once brought up by mining or drilling, the minerals will command new higher prices of the era in which they are separated from Mother Nature's earthy icebox. Bingo! You're even with inflation.

It is a pretty theory. But, like the gold-stock hedge theory, it has signally failed to work.

The reason is that in times of increased inflation, it costs increased wages to hire men to mine or drill. The drilling and mining equipment costs more than in the pre-inflation time when the hedge-minded investor bought his assets in the ground. The refining and marketing mechanisms need to be run on higher-octane dollars.

Texaco, Inc. is one of the world's giant asset owners, possessing and developing reserves all over the globe. If you had considered its stock as an inflation hedge in 1964, you would have paid about $3,850.00 for 100 shares (the high of the year was 45, the low 32, the average 38½). In late 1969, five years later, your asset investment would have shrunk to $2,800.00, despite ravages wrought by inflation on the grocery shelves, in land values, and even in the retail price of Texaco's own Sky Chief and Fire Chief products.

Bethlehem Steel, like Texaco, operates in many areas and possesses great reserves. A 1964 inflation-inspired investment in 100 shares of "Bessie," as Wall Streeters call this stock from its ticker symbol of BS, would have cost $3,700.00 at the year's average price (the high for 1964 was 43, the low 31, the average 37). In December 1969, you would have "hedged" against inflation by having achieved a $1,000.00 loss, for the stock had a price around 27 on the New York Stock Exchange.

Yet all stocks did not fare badly in recent years. Stocks are one of the things we will consider as a replacement for seemingly solid money. At the end of 1958 the Dow-Jones Industrial Average that most investors follow as a measure of the over-all stock market stood in the area of 600. Ten years later, as '68 rounded over into '69, the D-JIA was around the 900 level. An appreciation of 50 percent in ten years more than matched the rate of inflation, as measured by official indexes.

(But an average sort of performance was nothing compared to the pyrotechnics put on by the right kinds of stocks. In a succeeding chapter we will examine how people selected these stocks which performed so well in the 1958 to 1968 decade and how you can spot the right kind of stocks for the years ahead.)

There are no published yardsticks of real estate values as there are for stocks. But real estate values, too, appreciated more than inflation depreciated the dollar in the decade past. Land and buildings can probably do so again—as can other avenues for personally beating the inflation bogey which we as a nation do not collectively seem to be able to beat at all. The chapters which follow this may be your recipe for personal survival and success amid inflationary ruin of the uninformed.

TO RECAP:

1. The classic definition of inflation is more money chasing the same, or fewer, goods. When this happens, the inflated money supply pushes up prices of the goods and services. American inflation of the past decade began that way.

2. But after a while inflation, if continued, gets out of hand. Its causes need no longer be expansion of the money supply. Inflation begins to feed on itself as price increases trigger demands for higher wages, and these, in turn, bring on higher manufacturing costs, which, as the cycle progresses, bring about a new round of higher prices. And so ad infinitum.

3. There is reason to believe that present efforts to contain inflation will work but will only temporarily contain and not stop it, and that the fires will break out again. A conservative assumption is that the dollar might lessen another 72 percent in value over the ten years ahead.

4. There have been some terrifying inflationary binges in the past. No such binge is upon us yet. Still it might come. Therefore, smart people study the lessons of the past. They realize that, as individuals, they cannot stop the vast monetary tides of inflationary excess. But they can take measures to handle their affairs to compensate for lost purchasing power and to gain on the inflation.

5. In other lands and times, things have proved to be better possessions than money. Smart inflation beaters exchanged worthless assignats, Weimar Republic marks, and other currency as quickly as they could for land, cattle, castles, jewels, Volkswagens, stocks, and the like.

6. The same course applies to this inflation. The kinds of things have changed but the validity of the things-instead-of-dollars argument holds. Later chapters of this book detail

things which offer likelihood of continuing to function as alternatives for dwindling purchasing power of dollars.

7. But certain time-honored ideas for hedging have failed to work in the decade of the sixties. It is improbable that they will work in the new decade. Two such popular ideas were gold-mining stocks and companies which possessed inflation-hedge assets in the ground.

2
The Basic Strategy

"STRATEGY" comes from an old Greek word, "strategos," which in rough translation means "general." Strategy is generalship. You will need good generalship to get around an opening barrier to inflation conquest. The first—possibly the biggest—rampart blocking your way is taxation.

Therefore the first task of our basic strategy is to take you and your monetary forces around the taxation stronghold. It is better to go around this barrier rather than attack it in a straight line, just as sound generalship in war is so often based upon using a well-conceived flank movement instead of a costly frontal attack.

So we have two words to remember in this warfare to preserve you from inflationary ruin. The first, examined briefly in the previous chapter, is *things*.

Things such as land, castles, oxen—on or off the hoof—jewels, and even furniture help in the survival process during inflations. More sophisticated things aided the survivors of later inflationary binges in more advanced lands. The chapters to come will tell about things likely to bring you out on the other side of the abyss of *this* inflation with your real wealth, position in the community, and ability to enjoy life's better activities unimpaired and, if you are truly successful in your anti-inflation fight, even heightened.

The second words with which we must deal are *tax avoidance*. We are talking about avoidance, not evasion. This book is not a manual on how to beat a Treasury Department rap. It will go into ways to use the Treasury's rules and tax laws so you won't lose too many of your assets too quickly to the tax bite of a government which, itself harried by inflationary increases in its daily costs, wants to get in every buck it can.

The fact, surprising to many, is that it is as difficult for a government to survive bad inflation as it is for an individual to do so. Governments, too, find cost increases coming ever faster, but they, unlike you, are faced with a demand from voters for increases in services to those voters. If they ignore voter demands, they risk a turn-the-rascals-out movement at the next election. So Uncle Sam and his fellow governments of the West—perhaps those of the Eastern bloc as well—turn the tax screws tighter all of the time just so they can stay even and in office.

You want to get out from under the pressure of those tax screws while the tightening process is going on. It helps little to have an inflation hedge that works, only to watch the fruits of your success metamorphize into a tax payment, leaving you ruefully looking back on a year of effort with no real progress.

Thus your strategy is to own *things*.

And your immediate tactic is to *avoid taxes* on the gains from those things, to ordain the world so the increase of your flocks and herds will still be there after the tax collector has gone his way.

The trick, therefore, is to do one or both of two things in your planned conquest of Inflation Land. You must take profits in the form of capital gains, taxed at lower rates and, where possible, not realized until realization is unavoidable, so that as little as possible of even this lower form of tax will be incurred. "Realized" gains are those which you have converted into cash by selling things, as when you buy a stock at 20, watch it rise to 40, then take your gain by selling out. In such a case you have "realized" a taxable gain of 20 points per share, with the gain taxable at low long-term or high short-term tax rates as the law of the moment might dictate for the period during which you held the stock.

Ordinary income is not out under such a plan. Inflation may be a major problem for many years to come. You will want to survive and even prosper during those years, not merely pile up things and other non-monetary wealth against a day when inflation may have cooled but you'll be older and less able to enjoy the fruits of your inflation fight. Some income is desirable to supplement your continuing wages or the profits from your business or professional practice.

Moreover, there are ways to shelter some of the income from taxation. Even tax sheltering is not enough in an era of rapidly accelerating inflation. So we will plan to go after only certain kinds of very high income which are also possessed of tax-shelter features.

example If you make a 6 percent return from tax-free municipal bonds, this may seem good. But it is not high enough. For even without taxation on the income, there is the inflation bite. In a year of 5 percent inflation of the dollar—and we seem to have quite a number of such periods these days—your loss in purchasing power would be 5 percent, your gain 6 percent, your true "growth" only 1 percent, which is not a figure justifying much fuss, bother, or risk on your part. Better to try for the big yields above 10 percent, where, even after inflation, your true return becomes more desirable. Fifteen percent would be better, and 20 percent and above better still.

An approach such as we are outlining here needs some seed capital to get you started. Happily, a relatively small number of dollars can get you in, and if you are able to add to the initial capital from time to time, that is all to the good. "Small," of course, is not a measurable term. To a wealthy man, a small stake might be a half-million dollars. To most of us it would be a great deal less. It could be a few—and in many cases, a very few—thousand dollars. It is true that most of us don't keep sums like that lying around in an old sock or even in a bank account. But nearly all of us are able to raise it. In fact, everyone who is not a pauper can do so. Let's look at the ways to get this all-important seed capital.

In an earlier book, *Nine Roads to Wealth,* I outlined some of the methods by which an average person could embark on the big, leveraged roads to affluence. An important chapter of that book was titled "Ways to Raise Capital." It might be well to go over some of these, keeping in mind that not every way will apply to you, and that some of them might be more applicable to the man who already has considerable capital than to the one to whom "capital" is a word employed only by university economics professors:

1. A Bank Loan   Banks lend on all manner of security. Stocks and bonds are likely to get the largest-percentage loan values (70 percent to 80 percent on good stocks and as high as 90 percent of the value of bonds offered as collateral), and most bankers quote lower interest on securities than on other types of collateral. The reason is liquidity. If—perish the thought!— your loan were to be defaulted one day, a quick sale would repay the bank.

But don't offer a bank securities for collateral if your purpose is to get additional capital for buying more stocks or mutual funds—an inflation-fighting hedge discussed in Chapters Three and Four. Federal Reserve regulations set the "margin" rate which brokers can lend. Sixty-five percent is the rate at the time this is written, which means that the broker will be able to lend 35 percent while you put up the 65 percent. Banks cannot get around this rule. If you borrow on securities to use the money outside the securities markets, then the bank will lend you larger figures. If you borrow to finance more stock or mutual fund purchases, the banker cannot lend a greater percentage than the broker is permitted to lend.

It is well to know that banks' interest rates are negotiable. The first rate you are offered does not have to be the one you pay. Try the friendly bank across the street and talk to the friendly loan officer of the bank in the next block before you take the first friendly banker's offer. It is even permissible to try to play one against the other. "Pay one percent over prime? Not on your life!" you might say in friendly conversation. "The Swampland State Bank over in Dismal County will lend to me at one-half over prime." This isn't recommended, of course, unless there really is a Swampland State Bank in Dismal County and its folks will in reality lend at the better rate.

If you are a truly valued customer of the bank and possess a spotless credit rating, you might get prime. If they offer you a quarter percent over prime, they are being friendly indeed. One-half over prime is acceptable. More than that and it might be time to suspect that you are being treated as one of the peasants and that it is time to shop Swampland State over in Dismal County.

Bankers lend at better rates to customers whose other activities bring them profits. It is often advisable to cultivate good relations with one bank rather than spread deposits over several. "I'm big enough to be considered a worthwhile customer of my bank," a Western retailer told me, "but if I spread our activities over several banks, we would not be valued by any of them. Good banker relations are worth having during tight-money times."

But however friendly your bank relations, you should beware of two words when you negotiate a loan. If your banker offers you money at prime, that is good. If afterward he murmurs, "Compensating balance, of course," that is not good. Compensating balances mean that you cannot use all of the funds you borrow but still must pay interest on the whole amount.

example A borrower got $100,000.00 but agreed to maintain a 20 percent compensating balance. That would mean

$20,000.00 would be unusable. At prime rate of 8½ percent charged on the full $100,000.00, the borrower would pay $8,500.00 but be able to use only $80,000.00. His effective rate would be 11.6 percent.

Beware another word. This word is "discount." It can make the true interest you pay higher than you would pay at simple interest. Look at the same $100,000.00 borrowing. Assume a two-year payout on a regular schedule of $12,500.00 per quarter. Interest would be payable quarterly. The average amount owed during the period would be approximately $50,000.00. Simple interest charged on this would mean high interest payments at first, with interest declining as the balance declined. It would run approximately $8,500.00 for the two-year period, or $4,250.00 yearly on an average.

If the banker were to make this a discount loan, however, he would compute interest for two years at the full amount and deduct this off the top. He would then take $17,000.00 interest instead of $8,500.00. Moreover, since interest came off the top, the borrower would receive only $83,000.00 instead of $100,000.00. Payments would be made quarterly and the average balance payable during the period would be about $41,-000.00. A quick computation of $17,000.00 interest over two years—$8,500.00 per year—on an average $41,500.00 balance yields an interest figure of 20.4 percent.

2. The Small Business Administration Sometimes you can't get a loan through conventional channels at all. Your collateral may be insufficient or your operating history too short. If you are self-employed, or if you wish to try some of the business operation ideas discussed in later chapters—on either a sideline or a full-time basis—talk to the Small Business Administration, a federal government agency. And don't be unduly worried by the word "small" unless you already have a sizable operation. For SBA purpose, a small firm is (among other criteria) one employing fewer than 250 people. You can't qualify, however, if you are a subsidiary of a larger firm which doesn't meet the SBA yardsticks.

If SBA people are satisfied about the loan, they can arrange to get you about 80 percent. Part of this might be carried by the bank which turned you down in the first place but which, with Small Business Administration backing, is quite willing to take the now-lessened risk.

3. *Borrow on Insurance*   A sizable corporation recently reported that it was able to raise a half-million dollars by borrowing from insurance companies against the cash surrender values of life policies carried on its top executives.

Written into most life insurance policies is a provision for lending by the company against the security of funds already paid in. Most times, rates were set back in a day when 5 percent looked like high interest. They offer opportunity today to people who need funds and don't wish to pay the going sky-high rates.

"We don't have sizable cash surrender value in the policy against which I could borrow," a friend said to me long ago. "But with 80 percent of our needs promised from another source, borrowing on insurance assured the initial capital to swing our larger deal."

The steps above all involve borrowing. There are other ways to raise seed money. But before considering them, let's dispose of an idea which is deeply rooted in the folklore of American finance.

That idea, inherited from our long-ago Puritan spiritual forebears, is that it is evil to borrow. The old American ethic also held that a penny saved was a penny earned and that the thrifty fellow who socked away his pennies was bound to emerge in sufficient years as a well-off man of means. The inflation years behind us have proved the folly of the penny-earned bit in today's world. The dictum to beware borrowing is equally fallacious in that same world of 13-cent dollars and pennies which have become useful as sales tax tokens with no direct purchasing power of their own.

To fight inflation, do not be afraid of borrowing. Borrow to the hilt. Remember that a penny borrowed is—if inflation continues, as all of the signs say it will—only a half-penny you will one day have to repay.

That is the logic of borrowing in an inflation-harried world. As the money which has been borrowed decreases in terms of ability to buy worthwhile merchandise and services for your family, you will be paying back dollars of ever-decreasing real value.

(However, don't overdo borrowing so much that you're repaying big sums before the fruits of your investments ripen. Appraise your resources and liquidity needs carefully.)

4. *Don't Own—Lease* Leasing is a financing method which has the tax advantage of making immediate payments deductible where they would perhaps not have been to so great a degree under different circumstances. And leasing frees capital for other uses.

Thus if you owned land and buildings worth $100,000.00, and then sold these to a leasing company, taking back an immediate rental agreement stretching over a long period (this is called "sale-leaseback"), the capital formerly tied up in real estate would be freed for other uses.

This method of financing is ideal for the self-employed professional or small businessman. It is workable on another scale by nearly everyone, although not always with the tax advantage of immediate deductibility of expenses. If, instead of buying a car for cash, you were to lease it, you would have freed a sizable sum of money for ammunition capital usage. And if you additionally had a legitimate business use for the car, the payments made to the leasing company would become tax deductions.

There are other ways to raise the capital you need as ammunition for your fight against inflation. Such funds are in reality ammunition and we will call them by that name. Inflation is an enemy. A small or large capital stake furnishes you the ammunition with which to resist and, it is to be hoped, eventually overcome the enemy whose sign is the dwindling dollar.

The avenues for capital building which we will consider may not be usable by everyone. They apply particularly to owners of small businesses. It is worth looking briefly at them because, if they can be used in your circumstances, they possess the potential for raising vastly larger sums than you would be able to borrow or get by leasing.

5. *Venture Capital*   The search for venture capital does not necessitate standing on a street buttonholing passersby. Nor does it call for a long streak of wins at Las Vegas to get the money. Special companies invest venture capital. They seek sound investments in growing industries.

Sometimes, small businesses raise venture capital by "going public." The owners sell part of the corporate stock to the public. It is a tricky way of raising ammunition capital and, to be effective, should always be undertaken with advice and through the selling channels of an underwriter. This is a man who, in other circumstances and on other occasions, might wear the hat of an investment broker or dealer. He underwrites by guaranteeing sale of the issue (in most cases), and his sales organization peddles it to the outside investors of venture cash.

Going public brings a small business directly under regulatory supervision. An intrastate offering must be cleared through the securities authority of a state. An interstate issue goes through the usually more complicated machinery of the U.S. Securities and Exchange Commission. You will need help of an experienced lawyer and a CPA to go this route. But—if you possess a small business capable of going public—it offers more than the mere immediate raising of ammunition capital. By going public you establish a value for your remaining holdings and, instead of possessing so many buildings and pieces of equipment, you now have a marketable security for which public trading establishes a liquid value.

Running like a thread throughout these suggested ways to raise ammunition capital is our angle of *tax avoidance*.

When you borrow money from a bank, the Small Business Administration, your insurance company, or even your company credit union, and you then use that borrowed money to make more money through switching dollars into things likely to go up in value, you can in most circumstances deduct the interest cost from any income or appreciation produced by your inflation-fighting efforts. If you go public, you will probably not have incurred any taxable gain by converting a part of your business equity into cash with which to pursue other ends. Tax laws on these matters, however, change from time to time and it is wise to have the immediate, expert advice of a tax specialist, whether an accountant or an attorney.

In considering the sources of ammunition capital for carrying out our strategy of moving dwindling dollars into things likely to appreciate in terms of that inflation-nibbled currency, do not forget the mighty compounding effect of plowback.

example Let's say your ammunition capital purchased common stocks. How to choose stocks likely to appreciate faster as the dollar lessens in value is explored in the next chapter. Assume that you have read Chapter Three and have chosen wisely. The stock you bought for $2,000.00 is worth $3,000.00 at the end of twelve months. Your capital growth of 50 percent is a very enviable thing. This stock, let us say, also paid a dividend of $150.00 during the year. You can take the dividend money and buy a big dinner for your friends to celebrate your financial coup of the year or purchase some new clothing.

Or you might plow it back by using the dividend disbursement, an additional return on the invested ammunition capital, for purchase of more stock. Being a smart inflation fighter and more immediately interested in accumulating things than in spending dollars in celebration, you follow the latter course and purchase $150.00 worth of extra shares. Another year rolls around and at the end of it you are pleased to discover that your capital has again appreciated by 50 percent, thanks to your wise selection of a stock likely to go up in the latest year. The holding is now worth $4,725.00. It would have been worth only $4,500.00 if you had not possessed those additional plowback shares on which to go after further growth.

During the second year, thanks in part to continued profits increase on the part of the company and in part to your possession of those added shares bought with last year's plowback dividend, the company pays out $200.00 in dividends.

You plow that back. To keep things tidy and easy to figure,

let's assume another 50 percent year. (Don't think you will always be able to achieve such remarkable growth. We have assumed it here only to illustrate the point of how plowback makes a big increase even bigger.)

Your reinvested $4,725.00 plus the $200.00 dividend makes a total of $4,925.00, which is quite a bit larger than your starting two grand. Now add 50 percent to that. We have a figure of $7,387.50. And let's add to that the $250.00 which, by now, your company is paying. Your inflation-fighting capital has thus increased from $2,000.00 to $7,637.50.

Vurra, vurra neat.

And, of course, the longer you carry things into the future, the greater becomes the capital-magnifying effect of that important tactic of plowback. *Remembering that you must live now and keep up with present as well as future inflation, you may not want to plow back to this extent. A plowback to any extent helps.*

In mutual funds, as we will see in the chapter concerned with these swinging financial phenomena, plowback of at least one kind of disbursement is necessary, or you will drop back. Mutuals pay out two kinds of "income." One of these is true income. It is based upon dividends received by the fund. The other is usually called a "capital gains distribution." Unless you reinvest by taking fresh shares rather than cash, you will —using an investment sense of the words and not a tax sense— be spending your capital itself rather than the fruits and monetary berries it has produced. More of this in Chapter Four.

TO RECAP:

1. The basic strategy of inflation fighting is to move dollars of ever-dwindling value into things instead of concept money, with expectation that the things—as things did in earlier inflation periods and continue to do today—will go up in relation to dollars, perhaps faster than the dollars depreciate in purchasing power.

2. The corollary to this strategy is avoidance (not evasion, but legal avoidance) of crippling income taxes on the gains and increases of the capital employed.

3. This calls for eschewing ordinary income (in most cases) unless it is tax-sheltered. If ordinary income is so high that even after taxes it is greater than currency depreciation, this rule need not apply.

4. You must gather ammunition capital with which to carry on the inflation fight. Capital can be borrowed from banks, the Small Business Administration, or an insurance company. Remember about borrowing that, given continuing inflation of our already blown-up money, you will be repaying debt in a set number of dollars whose value will erode as inflation continues. In terms of purchasing value, you pay back less than you borrow under this strategy except in the event, considered unlikely here, that inflation should come to a true and final halt rather than merely subside only to burst out again.

5. There are other ways to raise ammunition capital, applicable more to the self-employed owners of business and, in some cases, professional services. These include leasing and the seeking of venture funds, often through the medium of going public by selling stock to outside investors.

6. Plowback is a mighty force. Unless needed, throw-off income from capital employed to fight inflation should be put back to work in the anti-inflation fight and not expended as received.

3

Stocks versus the Dollar

IF YOU LIVED through the disappointing and sometimes disastrous bear stock market of 1969 and 1970, you will find the statement below hard to believe. You may even find belief downright impossible. It is, nevertheless, as true as any prediction can ever be and it is based upon a set of conditions which are going to continue exerting influence for many years to come.

The statement is this:

Over the long term, common stock prices MUST *go up. They will probably go up faster than inflation dilutes the dollar.*

"Yeah," say some, "and how about that bad time during 1969 and early 1970? Did investors' stocks go up then? In 1966? In 1962? In others of the bear markets we have seen since World War II?"

The period since World War II ended is an excellent one on which to test our premise about bound-to-rise stock prices—remembering that we are not saying that all prices of all stocks must go up, but rather that prices *in general* must rise. During the post-World War II years we have had the worst inflation of this century. That is why those years make a good proving ground.

From 1945 through 1949 stocks moved through a sidewise trading range. The market wobbled back and forth without producing either a sustained bull (up) or bear (down) market.

Then over-all stock prices took off. Measured by the popular Dow-Jones Industrial Average, which most investors consider equivalent to market (although it is not) and as basic to the American scene as the Bible, stocks zoomed. They paused in 1953, but the pause was short and nobody then or now would term it a bear market. But 1958 was different. That was a true year of the bear. The high on the D-J Average was 520.77 and the low was 419.79.

There ensued a fresh bull market which carried the Dow, deflated in 1958, to a high of 723.91 by 1961. From there, it fell with a thud still remembered fearfully by investors who lived through 1962. The D-JIA dropped to 535.76.

But, nothing daunted, the market began another rise immediately afterward. This rise carried to a closing Dow-Jones Industrial Average level of 995.15 in early 1966. However, '66, too, was a year of the bear and the blood bath. Prices skidded all the way down to 744.32, nearly a hundred points under 1965's low of 840.59.

Yet, after that bad year, too, prices recovered and most stocks were much higher by the time 1969 became reality. True, the venerable old Dow average did not ever achieve a high as toppy as 995.15. But other market averages, such as the Standard and Poor's and the broad-based New York Stock Exchange Index, bubbled to higher new highs in early '69.

The point of all this is: Prices fell. But they always recovered and, on the average if not in every stock, achieved higher levels after each bear market.

The theory of ever-higher stock prices does not rule out

periods, some shortish and some of a year or better, in which over-all stock prices decline. It does call for prices of stocks to eventually recover. In the long run, stock prices have tended to go up, up, up. They probably will continue to do so. And as a result, common stocks are a sound inflation-fighting hedge.

The reasons why this is so can be summed up in two words. The first is *supply*. The second is *demand*.

Just as more money chasing the same or fewer goods will usually result in higher price levels for goods, more money chasing the same supply of stocks will create a situation which, over the long run, forces the stocks' prices higher. The money is demand. The amount of stocks to be bought represents supply. Happily for those who choose stocks as their inflation hedge, the probability is that proportionately more money has flooded into the stock market than into the economy as a whole. The odds appear to be in favor of a continuance of this pattern. The reason is growth of institutional investing.

A classic study of this situation was made by James A. McCullough, economist for the investment advisory firm of Scudder, Stevens and Clark. Published in July 1968, Mr. Mc-Cullough's study looked at only certain of the "institutions"— a term which to Wall Streeters means big conglomerations of investment capital from bank trust departments, mutual funds, fire-casualty and life insurance companies, and pension and profit-sharing funds. The group of institutions which Mr. Mc-Cullough studied included life and casualty-fire insurance companies, savings banks, pension funds, and state and local retirement funds.

Referring to the private pension funds, McCullough noted that at the end of World War II they held less than $1 billion in common stocks. "Today," he wrote, referring to 1968, when his study was prepared, "stock holdings of private, non-insured pension funds are approaching the $60 billion level and their net annual purchases of stocks exceed $5 billion. The total assets of these private pension funds by the end of this year will probably total $100 billion with assets carried at market value." The growth of other segments of the institutional market covered in the Scudder, Stevens and Clark study was almost as great in percentage terms. Continuing growth is projected into the future for all segments of the institutional group.

Assessing the supply side of the equation, which seems to guarantee a continuingly increasing (although from time to time erratic) level of prices for stocks, Mr. McCullough wrote:

> Just as the demand for common stocks, particularly by the institutions, has been inelastic, so has the supply of stocks been inelastic. We can identify a couple of sectors of supply of stock and, since they are so inelastic, we may have some luck in projecting the prospective supply of these sectors. One of these sectors is the growing volume of estate liquidation for which our guesses are shown on the table. About the best that can be said for these guesses is that our own broad contacts with the investment industry seem to lend some credence to them. The other sector of reasonable predictable annual new supply is the prospective annual sale of new stock by issuing corporations as part of the external financing of these corporations.
>
> Common stock sales by issuing corporations have rarely been of major importance. If we are careful to exclude the stock sales of financial intermediaries in 1928 and 1929, stock sales in the dollars of that period were probably close to $3 billion and $4 billion in the two years respectively. That was the period when the issuance of subscription rights reached its peak and the market was buffeted by some substantial offerings.
>
> Since that period, common stock financing has almost become a lost art as far as the big American industrial companies are concerned. By and large, they simply do not do it any more. 1957 was the last single year in which any appreciable number of large American industrial companies financed with common stocks. . . . In the ensuing decade, we have had a few issues by large industrial companies, significantly by the airlines and aerospace companies, and one common stock issue importantly by IBM. But that comes close to exhausting the common stock financing by large American industrial companies over the decade.

McCullough's conclusion after examining possibilities for panic markets is:

COMMON STOCKS
(In billions of dollars)

| Year | Certain items in new supply | | | | Some important institutional purchases | | | | | | Mutual funds |
	New issues	Estate sales	Converti-bles	Total	Life Insurance	Savings banks	Fire-Cas.	Pension funds	State and local retirement	Total	
1950	$0.8	$0.1	$—	$0.9	$0.2	$—	$0.1	$0.2	$—	$0.5	$0.2
1955	2.2	0.5	—	2.7	0.1	0.1	0.1	0.7	—	1.1	0.4
1956	2.3	0.6	—	2.9	—	0.1	0.1	0.9	—	1.1	0.5
1957	2.5	0.7	—	3.2	0.1	0.1	0.2	1.1	0.1	1.6	0.7
1960	1.7	0.8	—	2.5	0.2	—	0.1	1.9	0.1	2.3	0.8
1962	1.3	0.9	—	2.2	0.3	0.1	0.2	2.2	0.2	3.0	1.0
1965	1.5	1.3	—	2.8	0.4	0.2	0.1	3.0	0.3	4.0	1.4
1966	1.9	1.3	1.8	5.0	0.2	0.1	0.3	3.6	0.3	4.7	0.9
1967	2.0	1.5	4.4	7.9	0.8	0.2	0.3	4.7	0.5	6.5	1.6
1968E	1.5	1.6	3.0	6.1	1.0	0.2	0.3	5.5	0.5	7.5	1.7
1973E	1.5	2.3	4.0	7.8	2.0	0.2	0.3	9.0	1.5	13.0	2.3

E—Estimate

SOURCE: Scudder, Stevens and Clark

Having said this, it is still reasonable to assume that the growing institutional interest in stocks will be an important supporting factor for equities in the several years ahead. In this broadened market for stocks, yields and price earnings ratios are likely to be responsive to, among other things, the long range institutional growth and shifts of institutional purchases.

Added to this coming burst of institutional demand for stocks is the steady increment of investible funds in the treasuries of other types of institutions not covered in the McCullough study. Not least among these is the newest group of all. They are called "Offshore Funds."

These are funds which are sold to foreign nationals as a channel through which to invest in U.S. stocks. No one knows how much money they can swing. Estimates vary between $2 billion and $5 billion. The significant thing is not the present size of these funds. It is their rapid growth and the amount of added demand, in the form of Americanized foreign currencies, which they have the potential to slip into our stock market to perform the classic maneuver of chasing a more or less static supply of stock certificates.

More money. Static supply of stock. The equation should equal almost inevitably higher prices for American common stocks, always with the warning that bear markets can come upon you with suddenness, and, even though the very long-term move is decidedly upward for over-all stock prices, the immediate movement, unless you are careful about market timing, might be as disastrous as it was in 1962, 1966, and 1969. We will later study methods for trying to avoid such downslides.

But higher over-all stock prices do not guarantee higher prices for the stocks *you* buy. Not even if you buy the bluest of the blue-chip stocks.

For example, U.S. Steel, largest steelmaker around, sold at 108 in 1960 and down to the mid-thirties in 1969. That proved an inflation hedge in reverse. The giant General Foods, blessed with increasing per share earnings, slid from its 1961 high of 107 to a price of 80½ in mid-December 1969. The drop was not as searing to the finances of an investor as that in U.S. Steel. But it was hardly a safeguard against inflationary erosion, either. Examples like this can be pointed to by the dozen and the score. They prove this:

Over-all growth of the type projected by this study does not guarantee success. Selectivity and timing are of paramount importance. Many people prefer to leave the selectivity bit to the pros. These inflation fighters buy mutual funds. The funds and the inflation hedge they offer will be discussed in the next chapter. Other investors, however, say that they can do better choosing their own stocks, and that it is a lot more fun to do so.

Here are some rules practiced by the professionals which should make your selections safer, your gains bigger, and your sales and switches of stocks more timely:

1. *Choose Stocks with Growing Earnings* A stock's fortunes up or down on the board will ultimately depend upon the good and bad fortunes of the company in its search for profits. No corporation exists merely to jangle cash register bells. Many have sales that grow and grow—while the per share earnings figures stay stable. Professional investment people pay a lot of attention to the per share earrnings. It indicates the amount of net profit applicable to each share of common stock and is more important than the raw profit figures because, if a company's profits grow but the number of shares it has outstanding also grows, then the stockholders individually have no more equity in higher profits than before profits began to increase.

example Angleworm, Inc. has sales of $1 million per year, profits of $100,000.00, and 100,000 shares outstanding. The per share earnings are $1.00 per share. Now Angleworm's eager management embarks on a spree of mergers and acquisitions of companies in all kinds of fields, creating out of the buy-'em-up activity a junior conglomerate with sales of $85 million, profits of $2 million, and two million stockholders. The sales have increased eighty-five-fold. This is a very impressive figure. The profits, too, have increased. They are twenty times what the net profit figure had totaled before the merger-acquisition binge got under way. But, alas, Angleworm in acquiring so many unrelated companies issued a great deal of stock, and now, instead of having 100,000 shares, it has two million shares outstanding. Quick arithmetic shows that despite all the fireworks, publicity, and addition of far-flung new plants, a stockholder still has only a lonely buck applicable to each of his shares. Angleworm was a "growth" company only on the pages of a publicity man's release. In the eyes of hardnosed professionals along Wall Street, true progress was nonexistent. Hence a likelihood is that progress in the way of price performance has been unspectacular, too.

You look for companies with growing earnings per share. Some companies achieve this happy state by existing in growing fields. Corporations catering to man's added leisure fall very definitely into this category. There are all kinds of other growth fields. It is well to observe each carefully. For in many of those fields, the growth of competition will be found to have outstripped the growth of consumer demand. A result in such a situation is likely to be no real growth of corporate profits. This has happened in the air-conditioning field, where proliferation of competition ate up all the expected benefits of growth in demand and made the prices of air-conditioners become price footballs. It happened in many electronic areas. It will happen again in some areas which have not even emerged as growth opportunities.

The U.S. Dept. of Commerce has issued a study listing growth industries during the 1958–1968 decade. These were: aircraft; automatic vending machines; blast furnaces and steel mills; boat building; book publishing and printing; cathode-ray picture tubes; commercial printing (lithographic); computing and related machines; construction machinery; corrugated and solid fiber boxes; dental equipment and supplies; electrical housewares and fans; elevators and moving stairways; farm machinery; fiber cans, tubes, and drums; frozen fruits, juices, and vegetables; industrial gas cleaning equipment; industrial process controls; industrial trucks and tractors; jewelry and precious metal; knit fabrics; manifold business forms; man-made fibers (non-cellulosic); meat packing; mechanical measuring devices; metal-cutting machine tools; metal office furniture; motor vehicles and parts; newspapers; optical instruments and lenses; organic chemicals; paper mills; petroleum refining; pharmaceutical preparations; photographic equipment; plastics materials and resins; plastics products; primary aluminum; radio communications equipment; radio and television receiving sets; railroad cars; refrigeration machinery; semiconductors; special dies and tools; steel foundries; surgical and medical instruments; synthetic rubber; telephone and telegraph apparatus; textile machinery; toilet preparations; toys and games; trailer coaches; truck and bus bodies; truck trailers; and tufted carpets and rugs.

Investments made in stocks of those industries in 1959 and liquidated in 1969 would have produced some wonderful profits to an investor forethoughted enough to have envisioned the results of the U.S. Dept. of Commerce report ten years in advance. True, not all of the stock groups were good to those who invested in them. The steel mills' and foundries' over-all volume may have grown, but prices of the steel stocks did quite the reverse. However, there were enough big winners on the list—imagine a 1959 investment in trailer manufacturers or the makers of surgical-medical equipment!—to have made a broad-based investment in growing areas a hedge that not only kept abreast of the accelerating inflation of the sixties but decisively beat it.

That, then, is a criterion for picking stocks to beat the inflation of the next decade: stocks in growing areas.

But will these same stocks repeat? The answer is that some will, but you cannot depend upon industries which prospered during one set of financial, business, and social conditions to do so again—although they may.

Without pretending that I possess a crystal ball which can foresee what the USDC may put in a similar book in the late seventies, I would be willing to bet that some—maybe all—of the following industries might be among the wide gainers of the decade ahead:

■ Food firms which bend their efforts toward upgrading

food production in the less advanced lands where starvation is presently an immediate problem for so large a part of the earth's people.

■ Companies which tune their antennae to the needs of people, sensing the new social movements and the developing wants and moving to act in line with the future. I have always believed that a reason for the decline of the railroads during the two decades immediately after World War II was that they considered themselves rail companies instead of transportation companies. The result was that amid the most widespread people mobility ever seen, their passenger operations dwindled and died. There may be a resurgence ahead, now that these companies are beginning to look to needs instead of hewing only to their traditional ways.

■ Corporations which see people's dissatisfaction with pollution, overcrowding, and a beehiving existence and attempt to give us a cleaner, more individually dignified life in the next ten years.

■ Companies connected with space exploration. This is a dangerous area for investment, however, for knowledge expands fast and technology with it. Few of the space age technological leaders of 1960 occupied that position in 1970. But those which did prospered mightily, and small investments made in their stocks ten years earlier blossomed into fortunes for investors who chose the right space leaders as inflation-hedge vehicles.

■ Other corporations which see needs and not existing markets, and which are sufficiently flexible to change their whole way of corporate life if it should appear that such a change can serve humanity and benefit their stockholders in the process.

No matter what growing areas you pick today, they can cease to grow with suddenness and, for those stockholders not alert to change, with possibly disastrous financial results. So I offer this suggestion: Make a list of probable industrial areas of the future. It can be similar to the short list I have given here. It might include utterly different choices. Then invest as your judgment of new directions has impelled you to invest. *But be sure you invest in new directions,* for the world moves faster all of the time, and as man's knowledge grows, his outdating of existing technology and needs comes ever more quickly.

2. Don't Stick to Your Stocks with Too Much Stubbornness Make a new list every year. If additional growth areas offer greater promise than is now offered by the slowing growth conditions of yesterday, switch your funds into new stocks. You will make mistakes when you do this. You will sometimes abandon investments in stocks which soar to the sky after you have sold them. You may put the capital and profits of such a sold-out situation into a new situation which fails to grow at all or, like the air-conditioning industry cited earlier, grows into a profitless prosperity. You will be tempted, if that happens, to say: "Phooey. I'll buy 'em and hold 'em instead of doing such switching as this." Don't succumb to the temptation to take such an attitude. For mistakes are inevitable. The system of constant reappraisal is a sound one. It is much sounder than the system of buy and put away in the bank box, which worked well in our fathers' slower-moving times but which is less workable today.

Hew to your policy of picking growth areas and then reappraising from time to time to determine if growing-er areas might be more inviting. Only in such a policy lies salvation for inflation-harried dollars. Make your mistakes; accept the occasional losses; but don't abandon the system. If you implement it wisely, it will see you through the period of possibly faster inflation which lies ahead.

3. And Remember! We Are Not after Dividends With investments in the kind of growth-area stocks discussed here, dividends might furnish a drag instead of an added fillip to your results. This can occur if you begin to consider them important. Tell yourself, if such a state of mind arises, that dividends are ordinary income. Uncle Sam's tax-collecting computer takes away a large share of ordinary income. It does this even if you are not in a very high tax bracket. But capital growth—that is a very different breed of bird. That is yours until you realize a profit by selling the security. Then it remains yours in a greater degree than do dividends, since—depending upon the holding period set by tax laws changing as you read this—you keep most of your gain.

Dividends can get you into trouble. Remember, in regard to stocks, that you will pick them as inflation hedges (1) if they are in growing areas or (2) if the individual company has demonstrated continuing ability to turn increasing sales dollars into per share earnings increases. Given the stock of such a company, you should buy it if it pays a big dividend, if it pays a moderate dividend, if it pays a minuscule dividend, or even if it pays no dividend.

Make a rule for inflation fighting: Dividends don't matter.

4. *Watch Out for the Traps*   In the bad old days, traps used to be set for an unwary public by professionals called "manipulators." They "painted the tape" with appearance of activity and rising prices to tempt in suckers. Once these investors began to buy the stocks manipulated, the old-time con artists of Wall Street's earlier eras unloaded into the suckers' portfolios big positions previously accumulated. They did other things. They set bear traps and bull traps. They engaged in wash sales, with the left hand selling to the right hand. But they didn't set any traps as dangerous as some you'll find in the investing forest today.

Among these traps for the unwary is something that most Americans consider as reliable as hot weather in July and as wholesome as Mom's apple pie: accounting.

Non-accountants are surprised to learn that the books can say almost anything management wants them to say. Accounting is not an exact science. Its critics say it isn't a science at all. Some of the more bitter critics of the sharp-pencil profession say it isn't even an art. In the hands of some stock market people, bookkeeping has indeed become a trap—but a legal one.

The trick is not what they enter on the books, but how. In 1969, the stocks of wide-ranging conglomerate corporations that controlled operations as far-spread as movies and mining, auto trailers and automatic typewriters, came a cropper. Investors suddenly discovered something that thoughtful analysts

had known all along and that many of the analysts had re-
peatedly proclaimed to an unheeding Wall Street: the books
didn't always present a consistent picture of operations at all.
Although many of the conglomerates were solid operating en-
tities, as respectable as your Aunt Sally, they were tarred with
the brush that splattered suspicion on all conglomerate earnings.

Conglomerates grew because their earnings grew. The earnings, in turn, made higher stock prices. The higher stock prices
gave conglomerators necessary "Chinese money"—as sarcastic
Wall Streeters called this inflated stock—to buy up still more
unrelated corporations and start the process going again.

There are many ways to make earnings grow at a pencil
stroke. Depreciation periods can be lengthened out. Expenses
that most corporations charge off as they are incurred are
sometimes put on a long-time depreciation table to lessen the
cost bite, and hence increase the earnings, for a current year.
It was pointed out by one observer concerning two giants in a
growing field (neither a conglomerate and both conservatively
managed) that one consolidated all profits of its foreign subsidiaries so that these appeared as part of the parent company's
earnings, and the other brought into earnings only the dividends actually received from foreign subsidiaries. Both followed recognized accounting methods. But had Company A
kept books as did Company B, its earnings would have tripled.
Had Company B kept books in the manner of Company A,
earnings would have been nonexistent.

Accounting can make such a difference.

The trap for investors arises less from possible chicanery—of
which there is surprisingly little in today's investment world
—than from comparing companies' earnings without knowing
the differing methods which might make the more desirable
investment look temporarily poorer than another company
with which it is being compared.

"Hot" new issues are another trap. Periodically in Wall
Street a frenzy arises among investors. An idea takes hold that
small companies, new to the business scene but sporting sexy
names and engaged in activities too scientifically complicated

to be understood by the layman, are bound to prosper more than the established companies, often engaged in the same scientific fields and possessed of experienced, able management in depth. When that happens, as it did in 1961 and again in 1969, it is often a sign that a bull market of long duration is no longer a good bet to endure further. And it is a sign that many inexperienced investors are going to be poorer before too much time has passed.

A task force of New York State Attorney General Louis Lefkowitz reported in 1969 that their investigations showed "in only a small minority of cases did investors state that the prospectus had any influence on their decisions." In other words, the prospectuses—which by law must divulge all facts—were ignored and blind enthusiasm for hot issues became a major reason for buying them. The Attorney General's report added that "the typical language in these documents indicating high risk was largely disregarded by readers."

In some cases the traps into which inflation fighters fell when using stocks to better the dwindling dollar were of the deliberate making of unscrupulous operators. The United States Securities and Exchange Commission files show many of these. But in a majority of cases, traps are set by the investors themselves, who ignore facts but believe whispered tips and inside word given on the golf green, who select stocks because of pretty names rather than for expected results, and who refuse to follow the professional's prime rule of taking losses quickly and while they are still small.

5. *Leverage if You Have Limited Funds*   There are many ways by which the inflation fighter with limited ammunition capital can make it do the work of much larger sums in the stock market. Bringing about this happy result of possibly big returns from not-too-big capital is called "leveraging." Before you do it, you should understand that leverage is like a sword with two sharp edges. It can cleave your way through inflation. Or, if things go badly, the leverage can hurt you badly. This comes about because leverage magnifies both good and bad results.

There are many kinds of leverage.

■ The simplest is the use of "margin," or borrowed money. The Federal Reserve Board sets margin rates. Currently, these are set at 65 percent. This means that if you buy $1,000.00 worth of stock, you need put up only 65 percent, or $650.00, and your broker will lend the rest (not forgetting to charge you interest). Thus $650.00 does the work of $1,000.00. Margin rates may be different from time to time. They have ranged in the last twenty years from 50 percent to 100 percent, at which time no margin was allowed.

■ "Options" allow wide leverage. An option might be a warrant. This is a form of security which confers the right to buy a set number of common stock shares at a predetermined price. Usually, warrants trade at less than the value of the stock. They have no intrinsic value of their own other than the ability to command blocks of stock.

example   Company A's stock trades at 50. There are warrants, trading at 10, which permit purchase of Company A stock at 40. Say the stock of Company A goes to 50. The common has appreciated $10.00 per share, or 25 percent. The warrant must go up at least the same 10 points; that much value has been added to it, since a purchase of stock at 40 is now immediately worth 50 now that the stock has risen. The warrant, then, is at 20 and it has appreciated 100 percent while the stock itself went up only 25 percent.

Another kind of option is called a "Put" or a "Call." You buy one of these through your brokerage firm. A Call permits you to buy Company A stock, usually at the prevailing market price of the moment. You can have it written for thirty days, sixty days, or maybe up to six months ten days. Your fee for the Call varies with the length of time it specifies. If Company A stock goes up as in the example above, the arithmetic of holding a Call might go like this:

Cost of Call on 100 shares	$500.00
Rise in 100 shares of stock	$1,000.00
Profit	$500.00

You would thus have doubled your invested capital. But if the stock of Company A did not go up, you might have lost every cent put out to buy a Call. It is particularly frustrating to investors who use such Calls to see the stock sit stably and and staidly right where it started while the time period of the Call runs out—and *then* take off on the expected rise. When things go as expected, people who employ Calls dine on pheasant. When they go otherwise, Call buyers are sometimes lucky to have hamburger. The leverage is great. So is the risk. A Put is the opposite of a Call. You buy one if you expect a stock to go down. And if it does so, you can make money on your Put.

Up or down, it should be kept in mind that Puts and Calls are tools of the speculator, not of the long-term inflation-fighting investor. The warrant is also more a speculator's tool, but it, at least, has a sufficiently long life in most cases so that you can hold it for a longer period than a month or few.

6. *Consider Foreign Stocks*   Sometimes the stock markets in foreign countries experience faster advances than those of the U.S. This happened to the hot Japanese stock market in 1969. You face several hazards in buying foreign stocks. One is the Interest Equalization Tax.

This tax was imposed to "equalize" low American interest rates with the higher interest rates of other lands so that hot American capital would not flow out seeking the big interest returns. Our interest rates as this is written are as high as those in any advanced land and higher than most, yet the tax continues to equalize what is not any longer unequal. Probably its true purpose was to discourage any American investment outside our borders. You can escape Interest Equalization Tax if you buy American-owned shares. These trade at prices different from those of the shares which were not in American hands prior to passage of the tax.

Paucity of information is a hazard of foreign stock investment. You can overcome this by getting the people who are pros in foreign investment to choose your stocks through the purchase of mutual funds, usually U.S.-headquartered, which invest in other areas of the world. The next chapter will deal with mutual funds, and if you wish further details there is an earlier book of mine called *How to Make Money with Mutual Funds* (McGraw-Hill Book Company).

Many foreign securities are traded in the United States in the form of American Depositary Receipts, usually abbreviated as "ADRs." These are issued by banks and evidence the fact that the bank holds the actual stock.

Why trade foreign stocks? In 1969, Japanese stocks had a rapid rise while the American stock market was declining. Earlier, European Common Market stocks soared. In Mexico, there are sometimes stocks backed by assests, earnings, and dividends which make them big bargains in the eyes of many U.S. analysts.

7. *You Don't Have to Ride the Roller Coasters* If you can save yourself from the debacles such as those which came in 1962, 1966, and 1969, when all stock prices tumbled, you are able to make your capital purchase more shares close to a bottom. This is true even though, as we have seen, markets *do* come back. But how does an inflation fighter determine when a stock market is topping? Or when a weary, hurtful decline is about to bottom out?

Earlier, we have considered the ways in which the Federal Reserve expands and contracts the money supply and how the overexpansion of the money supply in the mid- and late sixties triggered the inflationary explosion. More than other parts of the economy, the stock market is fueled by money. A search for monetary series which appear to correlate with stock market movements has brought forth two that can help you increase the effectiveness of your stock activities by selling out close-to-top areas and buying back in close-to-bottom areas. These are called "Money Stock Plus Time Deposits" and "Reserves of Member Banks." To follow them, write the Federal Reserve Bank of St. Louis, asking to be put on its mailing list to receive publications which have graphic information of the kind shown in Figures 2 and 3.

The beauty of these two monetary data series is that they

tend to turn down when a stock market decline is going to be a truly serious one. They ignore the minor wiggles and fluctuations of stock prices. Thus, if a decline starts and these two go right on advancing, probabilities are that the decline won't be serious. Past performance is never a guarantee of future results. The two series might fail miserably when the next decline or advance begins. But they have a sound history. Consider the following:

The period from the 1966 bear market to the 1969 bear market was a very hard one for investors. There were peace hopes and war scares, easing money conditions followed by the greatest monetary stringency within memory of living people. European currencies rose (the German mark) and fell (most other currencies, with the notable exception of the Swiss

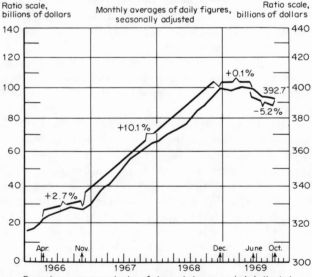

MONEY STOCK PLUS TIME DEPOSITS

Percentages are annual rates of change between periods indicated. They are presented to aid in comparing most recent developments with past "trends."

Latest data plotted: October preliminary. Prepared by Federal Reserve Bank of St. Louis.

FIGURE 2

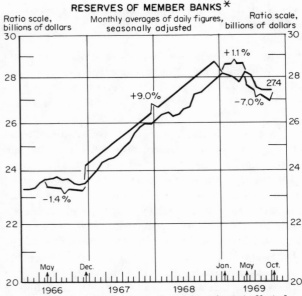

RESERVES OF MEMBER BANKS *

Ratio scale, billions of dollars   Monthly averages of daily figures, seasonally adjusted   Ratio scale, billions of dollars

* Data before May 1969 has been adjusted for estimated effect of reserve requirement changes and excludes increase in required reserves due to changes in regulations M and D, effective October 16, 1969.

Percentages are annual rates of change between periods indicated. They are presented to aid in comparing most recent developments with past "trends."

Latest data plotted: October preliminary.

FIGURE 3

franc) during this period. There was a hair-curling inflation in the U.S.

Yet an investor who bought in the early part of 1967 and held an invested position until early 1968 would have been well ahead of the game even considering the terrible inroads inflation made on his dollars during this time.

That is the course he would have pursued if he had taken our two series of monetary data for his guides.

"Money Stock Plus Time Deposits" gave a signal at the end of 1966 that monetary conditions were becoming favorable for stock buyers. It held to its favorable-for-stock-buyers upward track right on through 1968, with the seesaw market of that year's early months and a booming bull market during the rest of the year. Finally, this series indicated monetary conditions unfavorable to stock prices around the latter part of January 1969.

It is noteworthy that the series did not signal at the exact bottom of the '66 bear market. Nor did it catch the exact top of the '68 bull market. *Yet its signals were close enough to both turning points to make them of great potential profit to investors.*

"Reserves of Member Banks" gave its "buy" indication at approximately the same point following the 1966 bear market. At that point, the market was still full of bargains which were later highly profitable to those who purchased them. Many of the better go-go mutual funds were selling at prices which proved to be small fractions of the levels ultimately achieved in the two-year bull market which followed.

The warning indication on this monetary series came in the last third of February 1969. Again, this was not the December top. But again, it warned investors out of stocks at a time just before stocks began to seriously tumble in price and before the net asset values of so many mutual funds started to suffer.

8. *Pay Attention to Timing* There are two questions you must answer before buying a stock. The first is *what* stock to buy. The second is *when* to buy it. Each is important, for the right stock bought at the wrong time can mean that you purchased late in the feast when the smart people who bought at lower levels were unloading and you, with other peasants, are buying when smart money sells.

Many analysts employ a technique called "charting." They enter lines on a piece of chart or graph paper and out of the resulting squibbles they say it is possible to tell when trends change and to decide when or whether to get aboard young, new movements.

Other analysts answer, "Bosh!" These skeptics claim that prices of stocks are a random walk. They believe that prices are not influenced by tides of supply and demand, but tend to move up or down at random.

Among the people closest in touch with stock movements are

brokers. Recently, the *California Financial Journal* queried its readers on whether they believed chart study to be helpful in picking stock market winners. The December 2, 1969 issue reported results of this survey. The question was: "In predicting future movements of a company's stock, do you consider charting to be a very important factor, of some importance, or of little importance?"

Among the pros questioned, 56.1 percent said they considered chart study of some importance. "Very important," said 21.4 percent. Only 22.5 percent considered it of little importance. Thus 77.5 percent looked upon chart study as having validity of varying degree.

It will pay us to look at the basics of chart study.

Start by remembering that charts can no more predict the future than can tea leaves. But they do frequently tell the first tiny glimmerings of a trend change. Out of such beginnings come mighty market tides and, on many occasions, big fortunes for inflation fighters.

The basic chart study is "support and resistance."

A support level is a price area where one, two, and sometimes three, four, or five declines stopped. The more times a level has held, the greater the significance that can be attached to any eventual breaking of that level. You ignore any little level where the decline of Tuesday-before-last was stopped by some buying which came in around 1:30 P.M. It is better to look for the support levels which halted declines of many weeks. It is better still if they stopped declines of several months.

When a support level has been decisively broken through, you probably received a warning to get out of the stock if you hold it. Such a warning is not lightly ignored by inflation fighters interested in piling up capital gains to offset inflation's bite.

A resistance level is the opposite of a support level. It is an overhead ceiling. Bump, bump, bump go prices as they pound against it without going through. Every time the price of the stock reaches the resistance area, enough sell orders appear from the portfolio holdings of bears to mop up buying power and turn the tide at least temporarily downward.

As with the support level, you look for one which was able to stop an advance of some duration and size, not one generated by just a few buy orders. When your eyes scanning a chart book light upon a resistance area where many advances stopped but where a current one was able to slice through, you will, if you are wise in the ways of stock market timing, pull across your telephone and begin to dial the number of your broker in order to enter a buy order.

A *trend line* is not like a support or resistance level. It is drawn diagonally across a chart to delineate a trend. No advance goes straight up or down. Nor does a decline. Each has rallies (short up movements) and dips (short downward reactions). During an up trend, a chartist would draw a pencil line connecting the bottoms of the dips. During a down trend, he would draw a similar line connecting the tops of the rallies.

The big breaks in these lines often indicate the ends of trends.

From the reader over on the right side of the room who has his hand up comes a question: "What have I gotta do to maintain such charts as these? Spend all my time away from my regular business entering lines on a piece of paper?"

Happily, sir, you do not have to do this. You will find books of charts in nearly every brokerage office, available for your inspection and use. Also, public libraries often subscribe to chart services.

SIX QUESTIONS:

Q. *You discussed market timing. Some people say the Dow Theory is the only way to predict stock price movements. Will you comment, please?*

A. The Dow Theory is the oldest timing device around. It was worked out around the turn of the century by Charles Dow, then editor of the *Wall Street Journal*. That puts it in the timing race about where the water clock fits by comparison with a new all-electric watch.

But like the water clock, Dow Theory still works. Two

averages comprise the yardsticks that give its signals. The first is the Dow-Jones Industrial Average. The other is the Dow-Jones Transportation Average.

When the national economy is prosperous, both transportation and manufacturing companies must participate, since manufactured goods not carried to market are hardly in a position to sell, say Dow Theorists. An upturn touches both; a beginning downturn must affect them equally.

Theorists note that market movements come in three sizes. There are vast tides; there are intermediate movements lasting anywhere from a few weeks to many months; lastly there are the small daily movements. Daily movements are meaningless to Dow Theory except insofar as they make up intermediate waves, and these intermediates, in turn, count because they make up the big bullish and bearish tidal movements.

Any trend, state Dow Theory experts, must be considered intact until a reversal signal has been given. Such a signal starts when one of the two averages—assuming the trend has been upward—makes a top, followed by an intermediate reaction and then a new intermediate up-movement. The new movement, however, is tired; prices reach wearily for that previous high but they cannot attain it, much less exceed it. Now prices round over and drop into the next intermediate reaction. The reaction speeds up and, to the alarm of watching Dow Theorists, slices through the support of the preceding intermediate bottom. Half of a change-of-direction warning has been given. It means nothing unless the same thing happens in the other average to confirm this signal. Such confirmation need not come on the same day as the signal from the first average, although sometimes it does.

Sometimes instead of reversing the existing staircase pattern of prices, one average or both might move back and forth in a narrow trading range. Dow Theorists call this a "line," and a breakout in a new direction from a line has the same technical significance as the classic type of price action.

Q. *One broker says I should invest in growth stocks. Another advises me to speculate aggressively. I'm confused.*

A. Understandably. I, too, would be confused if I received the same advice. However, you don't really have a problem with stocks. The problem is semantics.

By "speculate" one man might mean the purchase of any stock more volatile than the most plodding defensive security. Another might mean the purchase of new ventures, of growing and risky young concerns, when he speaks of growth stocks.

Continuing to take a semantic view of things, you would do well to realize that you speculate whatever you do. The best investments can go down in value, the seemingly worst can rise to be tomorrow's blue chip. Once you realize that, you can then look at investing as a matter of choosing stocks by certain merits rather than because they have name tags pinned onto them.

Q. *A lot of money has been made in hot new issues. How do I go about buying them?*

A. With great care.

New issues have made money for some people. And they have been the cause of many losing their shirts—or if not the whole shirt, at least a few buttons and a sleeve or so.

The frenzy for getting in on hot new issues is a thing that seems to light on investing mankind at times of great speculative froth in the market. We had such a frothy market in '68. The present market in 1969 and 1970 appears anything but speculative and go-go-happy. There will still be times when money can be made in new issues. But go into such an issue, if you do, cautiously.

As for how to do this, the broker with whom you do business can probably get an allotment when you're ready, especially if the house for which he works is concerned with underwritings.

Q. *What are Treasury bills? Should I buy them? How?*

A. We discussed how to avoid the roller coaster's sickening down dips during bear markets. At such times you want to sell out of stocks, not watch them do a reverse inflation hedge by losing dollar value. At such times and given such strategy, Wall Street professionals usually turn to Treasury bills.

Bills are used by the government for short-term borrowing. The interest on bills consists of the difference between the price at which you purchased and par. Say you bought one three-month bill, which has $10,000.00 maturity value, at 7 percent annual rate. Your quarterly interest would then come to $175.00. The bill would cost you $9,825.00, and when paid off at $10,000.00 you would not consider the difference as capital gain for tax purposes, but as interest. So although no interest checks reached you through the mail, the interest was probably credited to your account by your broker.

Treasury bills are much in vogue among the pro managers of institutional funds during bear market years such as 1969. At such times, what is good for them can be good for you, too. Since the spring of 1970, they have been issued only in multiples of $10,000.00.

Q. *I can get advice without charge from my broker. Should I also pay for an advisory service or an investment counselor?*

A. Perhaps the group opinion of brokers themselves will answer your question. Not long ago, *California Financial Journal* published an opinion poll among the brokers' registered representatives who make up much of its readership. It reported that most California brokers found advisory services generally accurate and reliable. Altogether, 73.6 percent among the investing pros who were queried rated services fair, good, or very good. Only 12.6 percent rated them poor.

Q. *My life insurance policies have a cash surrender value of approximately $75,000.00, which is earning 4.5 percent with the company. Should I borrow any of these funds (at 5 percent) and invest in securities?*

A. Why did you originally buy the insurance, and do you want it as a benefit for eventual survivors or as something to bring you an inflation hedge or warmer income now?

If the former is your purpose, you would probably be ill advised to make a change. Any borrowing against the insurance would have to be paid back. Your beneficiaries might find your investments worth less than at the time you bought them—unhappily, this happens—and so the insurance payout would be lessened to meet the note.

If the latter purpose is yours, you might give consideration to reinvesting some or all of the policy.

4

The Mutual Funds That Whip Inflation

WE ARE MUTUALLY in great danger from inflation, and it is perhaps semantically a good thing that one of the best ways to beat this inflation which threatens us all is through a type of investment called *mutual funds.*

There is nothing new about the mutual fund idea. What is new is the way it has been applied in recent years by some young, venturesome, and on occasion fantastically successful managers who decided that the function of a fund could be more than merely saving capital from a loss so it could be passed on to Niece Jane. That is the kind of investing that funds traditionally did. These managers applied successful trading techniques to fund operation and some even invented good new ideas and methods of their own, with the result that some segments of the mighty mutual fund field have become very sophisticated weapons to use for beating inflation. Also new, and perhaps at least partly as a result of the swashbuckling concepts of fund operation, is the size of the mutual fund industry. Not so many years ago, the industry disposed of about $4 billion to $5 billion of Americans' invested funds. Currently, mutuals swing more than $50 billion, and during good years—years when the over-all market goes up—the sales of the fund industry in a twelve-month period are likely to be many times the size of the whole rancho back in the slower, less spectacular days.

Although they have been around long enough and are owned by enough people for most of us to know without definition what a mutual fund is, it might be well nonetheless to describe mutuals. These funds are vast poolings of capital. One investor might put in $500.00, another $5,000.00, a third $500,000.00. The money is lumped together and used to buy stocks. The fund gives each investor a certificate showing ownership of its own stock rather than of the corporations' stocks the fund holds in its portfolio. Investors achieve diversification in this way that many could not have obtained alone, so that their fortunes are not usually dependent upon the fortunes of a single company or a single industry. (But in some cases, to which we will come, funds deliberately concentrate investments in one or two industrial areas.)

Investors also achieve something more important than diversification, valuable as that is. They get professional management. In investing, as in dentistry, bricklaying, or football, the professional can usually beat the amateur. Unless you are well schooled in the ways of Wall Street, you are likely to be that amateur. Such pro management does not come cheap. The good ones command six-figure yearly pay, and a few get remuneration in seven figures per annum. Even the investor with a $500,000.00 stake can't often hire that kind of pro. But a mutual fund whose assets climb into the tens, and sometimes hundreds, of millions can do so. His services are what give a mutual fund the potential to be a good inflation beater.

It is well to review the kinds of funds you can buy, since not every kind is likely to be a vehicle for fighting the effects of dollar dwindle. (These were treated in detail in an earlier book of mine titled *How to Make Money with Mutual Funds*.) There are:

■ *Funds devoted to steady income.* Many have been very successful over the years in bringing dependable, sometimes even growing, income to their shareholders. Several income-oriented funds are "balanced"; that is, they include a mix of bonds along with stocks on the theory that if the stock market should decline, the bond market would probably go up. This strategy proved effective for many years, but when stranglingly tight money hit the country in the 1966 and 1969 bear markets, bonds often declined even more than stocks. Whether an income fund uses only stocks or seasons its portfolio with a few sprinklings of bonds, it is not for the man or woman interested in beating inflation. This is no reflection on the ability of managements of income funds, many of them able veterans who know their investing beans. Their angle is not one likely to beat inflationary inroads on our currency values.

■ *Geographical funds.* These frequently outstrip inflation. But they must be used with care and at the right times. Such a time was 1969, when observers could see that the economy of Japan was expanding faster than anything except the public appetite for pro football. From the beginning of 1969 to the end of that troubled year, shares of Japan Fund, investing in the rising Japanese markets, rose from $22.00 to $45.00 per share. This beat an approximately 7 percent rise in the Consumer Price Index.

Geographical funds do not always perform so spectacularly. The time has to be right (such a time was the year when Japan's tremendous potential shone forth clearly) and the circumstances also right (there would have been no rise at all without the reality of Japan's prosperity; funds devoted to other areas of the globe did not tend to increase during the bear market of '69).

Some geographical funds invest in special parts of the U.S. If you have reason to believe that offshore activity, oceanography, and food production around the Gulf of Mexico are in for a spurt, there are two or three funds which invest specifically in that area. Others cover different areas of the land of the free and home of the brave.

■ *Industry funds.* These can be useful inflation-fighting weapons. But the need to be right on timing and circumstances applies even more to these than to the funds specializing in certain parts of the earth.

In *How to Make Money with Mutual Funds,* I wrote:

> In a speech made during his short Presidency, John F. Kennedy remarked that "a rising tide lifts all the boats." While he was not applying it to the art of producing investment results, the thinking behind this statement is the basic strategy of a number of investors who say that when an industry is in Wall Street's favor, nearly any stock in it is likely to rise. Some will rise sluggishly, they admit, but all will eventually be dragged along for a ride on the tide of public favor. . . . today, many investors who value the industry approach have turned to mutual funds and rely upon sagacious professional managers to put them where the hottest action is.
>
> Some funds give the word "industry" its narrowest possible definition. . . . A growing group of industry funds managers today take a broader approach in the hope of producing steadier growth for their stockholders.

The trick with industry-approach mutual funds is to have them when an industry appears poised for growth, but to desert them quickly when that industry's growth appears to be over.

■ *Funds that employ special techniques.* Most good practitioners of a profession tend to have a background philosophy on how things should be done. Mutual fund managers are no exception. When a fund's management technique works, it can keep you abreast of inflation and ahead of the dollar dwindle. How do you tell? Look at a fund's past performance.

Some funds believe in the "technical" approach to investing. This approach relies upon charts, sometimes on computer studies. When an analyst using the technical approach knows his stuff, he usually produces the appreciation at which he aims.

Other technique-minded funds try to be leveraged with

margin, options, and the like, when they believe the market to be headed upward, and to reduce leverage, sometimes to reduce stock positions themselves, when they believe the market to be going downward. Analysts and managers of these funds may employ technical tools, look at background economic facts, or even use litmus paper (none do) as a test of the climate for stock appreciation. The ability with which the technique is applied matters more than the technique itself. If you like certain techniques, check the records of those using the techniques before you plump your money in any fund as an inflation hedge.

There is the hedge fund. This concept calls for a fund to be always both long stocks (owning stocks in expectation of a rise in price) and short other stocks (having sold them short in hope of a drop in price). The rationale is (1) that some stocks are always going up while others go down, so the investor may as well enjoy both sides of the market; (2) in sudden shifts of market direction, the fund will have its short positions as hedge on a turn from up-market to down-market, or the long stock positions to hedge a sudden shift from bear market to bull market. The bear year of 1969 should have provided a theater for the hedge fund idea to show off, since—in theory at least— hedges would have had great value then. Alas the hedge fund technique fell on its collective face during 1969, with some hedge-slanted mutual funds showing the worst records of that unfortunate year. This situation might change in the future; it is pointed out only as evidence that you should study the record of a fund before buying it because you like its technique or the way in which its manager's boyish smile shines in the four-color advertisements.

When ably run, funds with a special way they do their management thing can be effective ways to fight inflation. But keep in mind that from time to time techniques stop working, as did the hedge fund idea in 1969, even though it had clocked up several past years of success.

■ *New directions funds.* After the Russians launched Sputnik I into space, the U.S., in sudden fear of dropping back in a vital race, put on crash program after crash program to loft

Americans up beyond the wild blue and into the yonder above. Space stocks, electronics stocks, all kinds of stocks with space in their names and space for an aim, went up. Many moved faster than the rocketry the companies were trying to build. And so did the mutual funds devoted to new directions investing.

But new directions sometimes lead into blind alleys. Make certain that your fund is awake to the need for detouring from yesterday's direction into tomorrow's emerging new path. Check its portfolio changes as reported every three months, and watch whether net asset value of the fund's own shares is keeping ahead of the market and the dollar dwindle.

■ *Funds that buy other funds.* The idea of a mutual to invest in mutuals originated in Europe, where a fund salesman —turned big businessman—named Bernard Cornfeld began selling "Fund of Funds" to Europeans anxious to invest in the dynamic U.S. economy but not knowledgeable about which stocks or mutuals furnished the best vehicles. "Let us choose for you," in effect said salesmen for Fund of Funds. "Just as mutual funds offer you diversification and professional management for investing in stocks indirectly, we will add our own diversification of the funds themselves, and our professional management in choosing which funds will appreciate well."

Such a setup increases the cost of investing by adding another layer of commissions (funds pay commissions to buy stocks; investors generally, although not always, pay commissions to buy funds and management fees for handling the stock portfolio; under the setup here, a third layer of both commission and management fee is heaped atop the investor's back). It takes a lot of appreciation to eat through all of those costs. Funds that buy other funds are not the best of inflation-fighting tools. In that bad year of 1969, far from proving the worth of all those fees by investing only in the few other mutuals which showed appreciation while the pedestrian majority of funds were depreciating, one such U.S.-side fund declined in net asset value during the twelve months from $12.72 on December 30, 1968 to $9.54 on January 29, 1969. Capital loss of 25 percent hardly justifies a third cost layer.

■ *Dual funds.* These are closed-end funds (more on this

below) usually traded on the New York Stock Exchange. They result from an unusual concept in investing methodology. The dual fund has two classes of investors. To the half who have elected to invest for income go all of the dividends, etc., which accrue as yield on the investment of the whole portfolio. The investors who opt for capital growth receive no income whatever. But they get all of the appreciation and profits which accrue to both halves of the portfolio.

The point of all this is leverage. With 100 percent of the capital working to give income to only 50 percent of the stockholders, the income half of a dual fund has added financial muscle. And with all of the capital gains (if any) being added to the accounting of per share asset value of the other half of the combination, extra leverage muscle is applied to the accounts of those in search of growth. The income shares of a dual fund are thus meaningless to people who buy funds to beat inflation. But the capital growth shares can prove interesting.

But only at certain times and in certain funds. When a stock market is booming its way upward (remember the criteria for judging this which we discussed in the previous chapter), then the leverage of a dual fund adds enormously to the results *if* the fund is so ably managed as to produce capital gains for shareholders who elect this half of the whole. When a market is drooping and sagging downward during such a bear year as 1969, however, the leverage is all against you. You must avoid the bear traps in any kind of security investment, whether funds or stocks themselves. But it is doubly important to avoid traps if you hold a leveraged dual fund, for then the leverage which merrily produced profits will just as merrily bring about losses.

As vital as timing with dual funds becomes the matter of choosing a fund whose management has shown ability to beat the averages. You don't need the go-go-goingest fund every year. Good duals bring about growth of 50 percent in a bull year. Inflation does not proceed that rapidly. So you don't need the top performer. But you do need a performer. Check records during past bull markets before you plump your money in one of the dual funds.

Most of these fund types divide into groupings. Some are

open-end funds. Some are closed-ends. The open-ends have no set capitalization and the fund itself will sell shares any day you want to buy, or buy your shares if you want to un-invest. Not so a closed-end fund. These have set capitalizations just as do orthodox corporations, and once the shares reach the hands of the public, they are traded like other corporate shares. Most closed-ends are listed on stock exchanges. You purchase them as you would buy American Tel and Tel or the shares of George's Clam Juice Steak House.

There is nothing intrinsically better about the setup of closed-end than about open-end. Neither are open-ends better than the closed-ends. What matters is the record of a fund, the attitude it takes toward investing, and the success its management has demonstrated—or failed to demonstrate—in achieving objectives.

You pay normal stock exchange commissions to buy or sell closed-end funds. Not so in purchasing or disposing of the shares of open-ends.

Most of these assess a front-end commission called a "loading charge" when you want to buy. Loading charges can be steep. They often come to 8¾ percent. To obtain a share of the open-end load fund's portfolio worth $100.00 in terms of the current prices of stocks held in the portfolio, you'd pay $108.75. The loading charge is sometimes less and is always set on a sliding scale so that if you buy above a minimum amount (typically $25,000.00 per year), you pay a lesser load. Few funds charge for cashing you up. This is done at net asset value, which means the amount of all the fund's assets, less its liabilities, divided by the number of shares outstanding. Net asset value is computed twice daily.

You don't have to pay this loading charge. There are open-end mutual funds which charge nothing. These are called "no-loads." Some of the top-performing funds in the country are no-loads. But the existence of a loading charge should not be the sole criterion for buying or rejecting a fund.

example Here's a rapidly appreciating load fund. You might pay $1,087.50 for a $1,000.00 net asset value. But if the fund goes up 40 percent in the next year, you have run your money to $1,400.00, while with a no-load charging no commission but growing less rapidly, you might have only $1,200.00 at the end of the same twelve months.

The mutual fund industry is merchandising-minded. You can buy funds at X dollars a month, quarter, or year under plans that are called "accumulative plans" (these apply to open-end funds). A few accumulative plans assess a heavy front-end load which is different from the front-end commission loading charge, which operates on a per share basis whether you buy on an accumulative plan or not. Something has been done to reduce many of these accumulative charges. The Securities and Exchange Commission is apprehensive about the fairness of making an investor lose half of what he paid should he quit a ten-year contractual plan at the end of only one year.

The no-load funds have voluntary accumulative plans with no penalizing feature. So do many load funds. If you want to buy closed-end funds which are listed on the New York Stock Exchange (duals are among the closed-end funds), take advantage of the exchange's Monthly Investment Plan, which allows an investor to put in as little as $40.00 every three months toward purchase of fund shares. The MIP applies also to purchase of any individual stock listed on that Big Board. Like open-end funds' voluntary plans, the Monthly Investment Plan makes no charge for plans not completed; you can quit or switch at any time.

On purchase of a house, you can obtain mortgage insurance to pay up the loan if you die, leaving your heirs full and free owners of their home-place real estate. Mutual funds offer an inflation fighter this same opportunity if he buys on accumulative plans.

In late years, the emphasis has been on go-go performance among mutual funds. From our point of view as inflation fighters, this is a good thing. We cannot afford a slow 5-percent-a-year asset growth in a fiery era when the ravages of inflation equal and exceed that amount each annum.

But there are great dangers to the go-go approach. With unexpected suddenness, go-go funds sometimes cease to go and retreat backward instead. During bear years, which you want to avoid anyway (reread "You Don't Have to Ride the Roller Coasters" in Chapter Three), go-go funds' shareholders sometimes suffer fearsome financial wounds. One fund which led the pack in the bull year 1968 ranked only around 250 among 375 funds studied by a mutual fund rating service in the following twelve months. Even aside from the dangers of bear markets, the go-go funds face trouble when a concept or idea, dear to the heart of fund management, proves no longer able to cope with new investing conditions. The favorite funds of only a few years back are not found on "top ten" lists any longer, and it is a rare year which finds the top performer of the previous year still among the top five. It is more important to choose a fund able to produce steady performance of 20 percent to 30 percent a year than to buy a gyrating highflyer only to see it fall on its financial face.

In the portfolios of some go-go funds are latent torpedoes. Wall Streeters call these "letter stock." When you examine a fund prospectus, you might find them described as "restricted securities" and they might be convertible debentures or preferred as well as common stock. Letter stock comes into existence in this way:

Suppose you own a small factory with some stock trading lazily in the hands of the public. You need money for expansion. Securities and Exchange Commission registration takes time and costs a lot of money. You could seek to borrow money from a bank. But banks seldom handle loans for long periods.

Or you might sell some letter stock.

At this point, there enters a mutual fund manager. He says to you: "Your stock now in the hands of the public trades around 30 on the Midwest Stock Exchange. You want to sell another million shares. I will give you 22 for a million shares on a Letter of Investment Intent basis. That means I will furnish a letter stating my fund is purchasing the stock only for long-term investment and will not distribute or sell it in less than two years. You and I agree that at the end of 24 months, at our request, you will arrange registration.

"Our price is below the market for your present stock. But

if you sell another million shares, the price will probably have to come down, since you can't add that much to your capitalization without flooding the market. Moreover, you will incur high legal expenses and you will have to give the underwriter and his selling syndicate a good-sized slice for their services. Sell me the letter stock and you get funds now."

Thus, letter stock.

Funds have various ways to value letter stock. Most take it into the portfolio at the same percentage off market value that it was when bought, and it stays at that percentage.

example   Your $30.00 stock goes into the fund's hands at $22.00, or about 73 percent of existing value. If the marketable stock goes up to $40.00 per share, the letter stock is then valued at the same discount from market value. (It can be argued that this is a theoretical rise, since—not being registered—the letter stock cannot be sold at any price until it has gone through the SEC.) A few funds value letter stock at full market. That is, the $22.00 stock would go on the books at $30.00 even without waiting for the marketable stock to rise. "Performance with a pencil," sniffed one certified public accountant.

One fund heavy in letter stock had to stop redemptions of fund shares when trouble in the company and with its accounting methods brought about a stop in marketability for the stock. Later, the fund had to reduce over-all asset value by a large percentage as a result of loss incurred in markdown of this restricted security.

Another danger to mutual fund investing arises when a geographical fund's area no longer prospers faster than the rest of the world, or when the industrial segment of an industry-slanted fund is not longer the "in" darling of stock buyers. Only a few years ago Wall Street was convinced the Common Market concept had to make Europe prosper. The members of the Common Market did prosper, but not to the extent investors had expected. A result was that Eurofund, a closed-end investing in Common Market securities, sagged despite continued good management.

The lesson here is not to avoid Eurofund or other mutuals

of their type. You want to be in such a fund when its area is prospering and when the fund stock is showing great gains. But you want to watch for potential trouble so you won't be around if trouble comes or expected growth slows down.

Not all mutual fund investors differentiate between ordinary dividends and those which represent a payout of the fund's capital gains. "Gee!" said one investor to me recently. "I'm getting nearly 10 percent dividends a year from my mutual fund." He had combined the payout from both sources to arrive at this figure. You must know the difference and treat the two kinds of payout correctly.

Ordinary dividends are paid from the dividends paid to a fund by corporations whose stocks it holds. Say General Motors, American Telephone, and Amalgamated Spacetrot are in the portfolio. Amalgamated pays no dividend; it is a young and growing company anxious to use its profits for expansion instead of giving a portion to stockholders. From General Motors and American Tel, the fund receives $100,000.00 total dividends. During the year, it elects to sell its shares of Amalgamated Spacetrot. These cost $100,000.00. They are sold for $200,000.00, since Amalgamated, as noted, is a young and growing company with a significant stake in building space stations for further explorations of the galaxy, and investors, having seen its glamourous field and growing earnings, buy up the shares.

Now the fund has: $100,000.00 from ordinary dividend sources (this is the sum received from GM and American Tel stock) and a capital gain of $100,000.00. To comply with tax laws a fund must return all or most of such income during the year. Assume that all $200,000.00 is paid out to the 100,000 shareholders of the fund. They each receive $2.00.

The shareholders, unaware of differing natures of these payouts, consider both distributions to be yield for the year and happily go out to buy fur coats, scotch whisky, or other appurtenances of the good life enjoyed by owners of a mutual fund which is showing good results.

Smarter shareowners plow back the $1.00 capital gains distribution. In an investment sense, although not in a tax sense, it is return of capital itself, and they know that spending it as income would weaken their positions.

Sometimes very smart inflation battlers plow back both distributions, thus compounding the buildup of their capital by giving it a boost to higher total value on which to build next year's hoped-for further growth.

Plowback of this kind can be done to sweeten the buildup of capital in stocks as well as funds, and many inflation hedgers wonder: Why mutuals instead of stocks? If you feel adept in choosing stocks, but are also aware of the advantages funds' professional management can offer, consider what I have called the *50-50 Fund Idea*. Writing to investors not long ago, I outlined it this way:

> There was an old song whose refrain went "Ye take the high road and I'll take the low road and I'll be in Scotland afore ye." The 50-50 Fund Idea is a plan for taking two hopefully high roads with the aim of getting, not necessarily to Scotland, but to a state of greater affluence than anyone who takes only one road.
>
> It calls for investing 50% of capital in common stocks—not just any equities but common stocks chosen with the hope of performing notably in the early future and bought at a time and a price which analysis seems to indicate has minimum risk coupled with maximum potential. It calls for investing the other 50% of capital in mutual funds. But not just any mutual funds. Here, too, the 50-50 Fund Idea calls for selecting funds carefully on their promise of beat-the-market performance over months ahead. There is nothing static about the 50-50 Fund Idea, for as a stock or a mutual fund might falter it should be replaced with one that appears to offer greater promise.
>
> The common stocks should meet a number of exacting tests. Each must be a company with good potential to grow rapidly, through exploitation of a scientific or sociological breakthrough, through special internal conditions, better-than-average demonstrated management ability, or perhaps a developing new situation. Each must have demonstrated better-than-the-market relative strength (Momentum). Each should be in a buying area.
>
> Mutual funds, to qualify for the 50-50 Fund approach, must have shown ability to increase net asset value steadily from year

to year over half a decade. A stopped clock is right twice a day; similarly, a fund with one besetting policy or idea can be right if the fickle sun of Wall Street shines on it during one year, while being out in the cold the rest of the time. Look, therefore, for ability to increase asset value a minimum of 20% annually COMPOUNDED since five years bring many kinds of market conditions and the ability to grow in all is important. But that is not the only test: an important consideration is the growth of asset value over the past six months.

Thus the 50-50 Fund Idea gives an investor the best of both worlds; a package of common stocks chosen for hope of rapid run-up and mutual funds whose managements show ability to steadily beat the average for their shareholders.

SIX QUESTIONS:

Q. *Where can I get a list of no-load funds?*

A. The *Wall Street Journal* and most bigger-city newspapers carry daily listings of mutual fund "bid" and "ask" prices. The bid price is the net asset value of the fund at the latest computation. The ask price is net asset value with front-end commission added.

It is easy to spot the no-loads. They are the funds which have the same dollar figure for both bid and ask.

Q. *There are many funds listed on the New York Stock Exchange. How do I tell the dual funds from the rest of the closed-ends?*

A. I hope that after reading the chapter on funds you wouldn't be so foolish as to buy a dual fund—or anything else—without checking. If you read reports and literature about the fund, you will run into the words "dual" or "dual purpose." By all means check, for even if you get a dual, you won't necessarily get the best performer among this leveraged group. See what management has been able to do in good market years and bad.

Q. *I am not satisfied with the way the professional manager of our mutual fund handled things in a recent market drop or his timing in getting in or out of stocks he bought in an effort to make a capital gain. What can I do about it?*

A. The professionals who manage mutual funds are much like any other professionals, including those who practice dentistry, law, or medicine. They are not all equally good. Possession of a degree doesn't make anyone an expert. Something inside him helps, too.

And so it may be that your mutual fund's manager goofed. But it may also be that he was caught up in something he couldn't help. You as an individual investor can buy stocks, sell them when you believe they might be headed down, and buy others to replace them. He can do this, too, in managing his much larger portfolio. But you can do something he cannot. You can sell all of your stocks if you become convinced that a serious drop such as those of 1969, 1966, and 1962 is on the way.

He cannot.

He handles too much money to be that mobile with all of it.

If he and other professionals handling mutual funds were to correctly foresee such a decline as that we witnessed in '69, there just aren't enough doors for all of them to crowd out. Total value of mutual funds at the start of 1969 was around $53 billion. That constitutes a lot of share certificates. Dump them all suddenly on the market—and who buys? If fund managers did dump, the serious 1969 bear market would have become a financial catastrophe. Even 1929, 1930, and 1931 saw nothing to match what such a flood as that might have swept away.

Thus mutual funds generally fare a bit worse than the market in years of declining trends in stock prices. The ably managed ones usually bounce back fast, with better than market appreciation in the years of market advance which follow.

Your bet is not to be in funds at all when the market is sinking.

Q. *As an alternative to selling out when I am dissatisfied with the way the fund managers operate, couldn't I try to vote them out in a proxy contest?*

A. You could try. But you probably wouldn't succeed.

The mechanics of a proxy contest are staggering. Cost in SEC filings, in legal help, in publicity, propaganda, and just plain dirty in-fighting would probably wreck both your financial resources and your nervous system. Proxy fights are put on by big stockholders who aim, not at reforming management, but at getting control of the ranch and running it their way. If you fall into that classification, go ahead. Most of us find it easier just to switch funds, save money, and sleep soundly at night.

Q. *How much difference does a fund's approach make?*

A. Comparisons are tough in a book which might be read long after the answer is written. So I'll take three very real funds but disguise them as Fund A, Fund B, and Fund C in order to illustrate difference in approach.

Fund A is a front-end load fund whose approach involves the search for little-known small companies. The approach served it well. It was top dog among the performance funds in one recent year, and for several other years was among the top group. Fund A fell upon evil days in the 1969 bear race, however, with a serious drop in asset value from January to December.

Fund B is a closed-end listed on the New York Stock Exchange. It invests in the broad economy. Buying Fund B is a little like buying the Dow-Jones Industrial Average, because this fund invests in the same sort of blue-chip stocks that comprise the venerable Dow. It will go up about as well as the over-all market, and down about as badly in the off years. As an inflation hedge it is less likely to stumble than the go-go-ers but less likely to produce big results.

Fund C is a no-load open-end. Its approach is based on expected probability of inflation, and its stocks—while not always the kind of growth equities found in Fund A's portfolio—are those which its management expects to beat inflation. The fund is relatively new and therefore not easy to judge.

Q. *I have four children to educate and I can count on college costs going up faster than sirloin steak or truck parts. Will mutual funds close the gap between what I have available now and what the universities will require when my children enter their gates?*

A. You can count upon day following night, and figure on a strong probability of winter succeeding fall each year. Also, as Benjamin Franklin said, death and taxes. But not much else.

However, the probabilities are that funds, wisely chosen, switched when their performance begins to slip, and added to by proper plowback, will probably see you through. When Johnny, Susan, Tancred, and Gwendolyn go through those gates, they may do so on auto wheels bought with mutual fund appreciation instead of afoot.

5

The Real Estate
Rapid Express

ON THE WEST BANK of the Mississippi River opposite New Orleans lie the small towns of Gretna, Harvey, McDonoughville, Marrero, and Westwego. Recently an expressway was constructed to connect them and a new bridge was built across the Father of Waters. Results were predictable. The West Bank boomed, and once-sleepy little towns became bedroom suburbs for the expanding city. Fortunes were made in the land around these towns as swamps were filled, streets laid out, and houses built. West Bank property owners grew rich.

But not all of them.

Until the West Bank Expressway was constructed, an artery connecting the small towns had run alongside the levees. Plants were there, businesses gravitated to the river road, and the hamlets sprawled out from them like the folding fans our grandmothers used to keep themselves cool in a ladylike way before air conditioning or electric fans had been invented.

Even today land along the formerly vital river road is worth little more than it was a decade ago. Growth of the West Bank bypassed this property—once the choicest—but inflation did not bypass the property owners, whose groceries, services, and goods mounted in cost while their seemingly promising land lay outside the growth pattern.

There is a lesson here. Land, say people who deal in it, is the traditional builder of fortunes. Those who make this statement are correct. But all land does not appreciate. If you are going to fight inflation with land, buildings, and other real estate, you have to be able to differentiate. You can't win the fight against the dwindling dollar with river road land. You have to join the expressway boys.

Although land almost must go up in price over the years, all land won't go up any more than all common stocks are bound to rise because of the beefed-up institutional demand for stocks that was discussed in an earlier chapter. As with stocks, demand for raw land is being institutionalized today in vast pools of capital. These pools semi-guarantee that the land you buy—provided you choose the expressway and eschew the river road—will bring a profit. Maybe it won't do so tomorrow. But it will eventually, and perhaps that demand will grow to be so great that even river road land will one day soar.

The capital pools are sometimes corporate; sometimes they comprise the money of land companies which buy big tracts, promote them, and sell land in small hunks for home or resort lots. Typical of the former are such non-real estate companies as Westinghouse Electric, Weyerhaeuser Co., and other corporations that find land development a profitable use for capital not immediately needed in regular business. Typical of the latter group are a number of land companies, often with stock that is trading on the exchanges, whose business is buying cheap and selling dear. Even Investors Overseas Services, Geneva-headquartered parent company of Fund of Funds, which was mentioned in the preceding chapter—before recent difficulties—had entered the land development field with $67 million beginning capital to be put into raw land for development and resale.

All this adds up to a lot of money. The move to institutionalize real estate investing is newer than the institutionalizing of stock market money. Opportunity exists for locating land early with the idea of resale to the big buyers. The key to everything is foresight, embodied in answers to questions such as these:

1. Is something afoot? Can I logically envision the coming of a new development which will increase the value of this land in the future over what it is today without my having to invest anything except mortage payments in the interim?

2. Can value be added to this land? It may look like swamp or desolate mountainside now. But if a usable idea can bring extra value, then you can beat inflation with raw land.

3. Is a city expanding in the direction of my proposed land purchase?

4. Has this land a potential industrial use due to its proximity to water, transportation, markets, raw material source, or skilled labor?

There is a great deal of money to be made—more than enough to overcome inflationary inroads on your lessening currency—in buying and reselling raw land. There is still more to be made by developing that land yourself. People of moderate means can do this, thanks to the leverage of borrowed money. In this chapter, we will discuss both land and the things which can be put up on it.

Raw Land

Most people think of inflation-fighting opportunity in land in terms of semirural or altogether unused land of the sort that appreciated so much in value on the Mississippi West Bank opposite New Orleans. But there is opportunity in urban land, too.

Americans today are justifiably aroused over housing part of our population in what one sociologist has described as pigsties. Decent minimum standards in our cities call for tearing down the substandard buildings, and in that process many entrepreneurs have found opportunity to aid their fellow humans and at the same time hedge against the dwindling values of money.

Deploring some obstacles which stop private enterprise in New York City—many such obstacles unique to that city—Dr. Frank S. Kristof of the metropolis' Housing Development Administration noted in a paper given November 18, 1967 before the Conference of the New England Region, "Problems of a Mature Economy":

> Since public assistance to rehabilitation in New York City, aside from raising buildings to code standards, consists of removing major impediments to proper management of properties—such as burdensome taxes and rent ceilings that inhibit proper maintenance—it is to be hoped that the discouraging signs now apparent in the city's depressed areas can be reversed.

It is possible for investors of moderate (although not of small) means to get aboard the rehabilitation tide that will probably surge over most cities in the next ten years. Aside from this, there are individual opportunities in upgrading parts of neighborhoods, even single houses. More on this shortly.

Much mass rehabilitation will entail an effort to locate industries close to ghetto and former ghetto areas where residents of these areas can find employment. Raw land suitable for industrial use should be gobbled up as this effort proceeds. Writing in the *New England Economic Review* of January–February 1969, Carol S. Greenwald and Richard Syron noted in regard to job opportunities in Boston's urban core that in the Roxbury area,

> As of July, 1968, 29 vacant sites, totalling about 1.7 million square feet (39.3 acres) were zoned for industry in this area. Most of the unoccupied land was located in the South End. While the total amount of vacant land was substantial, the individual vacant parcels were quite small. . . . Few firms will consider a site less than two acres, and if allowance is made for expansion, most will want more than five acres.

The lesson: You can't build a plant on a single vacant lot. If you seek land to sell later for industrial use, buy enough of it.

To get a grasp of the inflation-fighting profit potential of built-up, overcrowded, sometimes garbage-filled, and usually traffic-clogged urban property, read what Grace Milgram and Christine Mansfield of the U.S. Department of Housing and Urban Development wrote in a 1967 study called "The City Expands." Reporting on developments in the city of Philadelphia from 1945 to 1952, they noted:

> The development which has taken place has been accompanied by an increase in average price per acre. Expressed in current dollars, there has been a 13-fold increase in 18 years, from $1,030.00 per acre to $13,300.00 per acre. . . . in deflated dollars, the increase has been seven-fold, from $1,350.00 to $10,250.00. Price of residential land has risen only slightly less, from $1,400.00 to $10,100.00 in deflated dollars, an annual rate of 14.5 percent.

Opportunity? You bet. Inflation doesn't go that fast. Not yet, anyway.

Suburban land offers some even juicier possibilities over the inflation-infested years which probably lie ahead of us. More and more people are moving into the countryside to overcrowd the once peaceful suburbs and to found new, farther-away suburbs in their drive to get a little grass-covered land around their habitations, a little more modernity in their houses, and such appurtenances of the better life as swimming pools, beach fronts, and country club memberships that do not involve 40-mile trips out of the asphalted areas.

There's a trend in the U.S. for fewer farm people to feed more and more non-food-producing people. A factor has been the increasing size of the farms as university-educated farmers put the economies of scale to work on the back forty. This has been made feasible by increased mechanization as tractors replaced Old Dobbin and bigger and better mechanized equipment replaced the first tractors. The U.S. chemical industry helped by making cheap, effective fertilizers to use instead of manure and compost. Each step meant that fewer farmers could produce more food.

"World starvation? Nonsense," one agriculture professor told me. "Gloomy people foresaw that sort of thing long ago. They said we would starve in the twentieth century. We didn't. Apply all the things we have learned in North American agriculture to the hungry parts of the world and their problem is likely to be surplus rather than scarcity."

Today sons and grandsons of people who long ago deserted the soil for the city are streaming back to that soil. But not as farmers. As suburban builders and dwellers.

The criteria which apply to choice of urban raw land apply in the suburbs as well, and in the forests, fields, and marshes that you hope will one day become suburbs. Smart inflation fighters look for a plan or project which will enhance the usability of nearby areas. They search for ways in which value can be added to land; sometimes this value can consist of no more than a concept salable to someone who is able to bring the idea to fruition. They look, too, for probable directions of city expansion; in many areas the wild countryside of only ten years ago is the settled, manicured metropolitan periphery of today. Possible industrial usability enhances the value of land out in what was once called "the sticks."

But buy land that you know, can see, touch, and smell.

Many an inflation-worried investor has purchased land in far-distant states, only to find that his lush oasis existed in the mind of a promoter and that the area, pictured as having utilities and awaiting only an imminent influx of new residents to bloom, was instead desert filled with Joshua trees and scrub.

If despite this warning you feel impelled to take a flyer in that parcel of suburban paradise pushed by long-distance phone, then you should know the rules governing interstate land purchase. Irked by shady practices of a small minority of land sellers, Congress in 1968 passed a law to protect the public. Under this law you have a right to demand from the seller whether he has a Statement of Record filed with the U.S. Department of Housing and Urban Development. Ask, too, for the Property Report, similar to prospectuses furnished to buyers of new securities. The law also provides that you must be told the distances to nearby communities; whether there are liens on the property; whether contract payments will be placed in escrow; availability of recreational facilities; present and proposed utility services and charges; number of homes currently occupied at the time you buy; if there are soil or other foundation problems; and the type of title you will receive.

When buying land, the old real estate dictum is true: "Well bought is half sold." Buy it at the right price and time, and you are likely to be on your road to an eventually profitable sale.

Good, bargain land is not found every day in the week. When you have the right piece, buy as much as the seller and your pocketbook will permit. Happily, real estate can be purchased with relatively little money down and terms stretching over long periods. You possibly won't want to hold the land for twenty or thirty years. But you will want to make minimum payments out of current income while your land's values (you hope) build up. With low downpayments and low regular disbursements you can swing bigger parcels of land than if you had to pay cash. We will look shortly at sources of borrowed money to provide this kind of leverage.

Improving the Land

Remember the concept of value added in appraising raw land to determine whether it might in future zoom like property along the West Bank Expressway opposite New Orleans or placidly stay in the status quo as did seemingly better land alongside the ancient river road. If you can do that value addition yourself, you stand to make bigger gains than by merely buying, holding, and selling plots of earth.

It takes more money to swing deals such as apartment buildings, office buildings, and shopping centers. But the rewards are in proportion. Statistics show that the share of the construction dollar taken by one-family dwellings has been getting smaller over the past decade. Apartment construction receives the greater part of attention these days. If you go that route, you are where the action is.

Many knowledgeable people believe the hottest part of the action will be in condominiums. A growing part of condominium usage may be—not for homes—but for offices.

The condominium is a cooperative building. Each man owns his apartment or his office. He possesses this outright just as he would own a plot of land and the building on it if he were an ordinary kind of homeowner with the traditional brick ranch house in a suburb. But he doesn't own the plot—just the living space. The land, hallways, and other cooperative areas are owned by the group together. Say you have a condominium apartment. Eighty-four other persons inhabit the structure. You own, in addition to the pad, one-eighty-fifth of the hall, the same share of the elevators, the elevator shafts, the ligustrum bushes in front of the front entrance, and the grassy land out to the sidewalk. Your ownership can be taxed. It is probably mortgaged—whose pad isn't? You can give it to your wife, leave it to your children, donate it to your favorite charity, or, in the tradition of a Suthun plantation owner in the old riverboat movies, lose it in a poker game should that be your bent.

To an inflation fighter, a condominium has some strong advantages over other kinds of buildings. This holds true whether it is the familiar kind of apartment condominium or one of the newer ones slanted toward office use. Consider:

1. You quickly recover a large part of costs plus, possibly, a sizable profit through sale of condominium units.

2. You can, if you wish, retain parts of the structure for your own use, waiting for it to appreciate in value as the dollar dwindles. You can, moreover, organize a company to contractually handle building clean-up and maintenance for the condominium owners.

The legal requirements for selling condominium space become complicated in most states. How complicated will depend upon local laws; your attorney should be consulted. In some areas the documents to be filed become as cumbersome and numerous as the filing requirements for a new securities offering of a company going public.

If you want to fight inflation on a really ambitious scale and can swing the initial capital as well as borrow necessary long-term moola, you might consider construction and sale of whole model cities. Birth and growth of a typical model-city project was described in the January 1969 issue of *Buildings:*

> When Palmetto Expressway doglegged around the Graham dairy property in the 50's, the three Graham sons, Philip, William and Robert, decided to attempt a planned community. Working within the Dade County masterplan, the new community would be joined to metropolitan Miami by an extensive freeway system, but self-contained for better, more pleasant urban living. It would utilize Metro Services for water, sewage, garbage collection, fire and police protection whenever feasible, but through careful planning the Grahams hoped to avoid urban problems of crime, ugliness and traffic congestion.
>
> Robert Graham, Harvard trained lawyer who serves as state representative, explains . . . Sengra Development Corporation and Miami Lakes. . . . "It was a combination of several factors. First, we had a situation just north of us where the owner took the fast way out by selling to a developer, but ended up with heavily mortgaged property and ugly little houses back on his hands when the developer didn't carry through.
>
> "Secondly, we had long experience with this place. Dad had owned it since the late 20's. We had an obligation to do something here other than reproduce what was going on in the rest of the area.
>
> "Thirdly, a friend of Phil's in California had taken the option of selling off to a developer. Unhappy with the results, he told Phil, 'If you ever have the opportunity to sell off and walk out, don't.' "

The Graham brothers decided Miami Lakes would differ from most new towns in two respects. First, it would be located far enough from the established metropolitan area to allow planned growth, but close enough to reach easily while the new town was growing. This would allow residents to commute while industrial and business sectors expanded. Secondly, growth would come gradually and naturally, like an agricultural crop, without moving in a total population and all urban services immediately.

On a less sizable scale than model community development or the building of condominiums is what some real estate people term the "remodel and resell" market. You buy an old, run-down house, make it a better one, and sell out at a profit. As such, this kind of inflation fighting involves operating real estate as a business—it can be a sideline one—rather than merely holding for the years and the inroads of inflation to lift the number of dollars a parcel of land or a pile of wood, concrete, and steel might be worth.

There are two ways to tackle remodeling and reselling. The first is to upgrade a house. The second is to upgrade a street or a block.

If you're going to upgrade a house, you should:

■ Look for a house that is rundown, dilapidated, and on the market as distress merchandise, but in a good neighborhood. The key to success will be in lifting the structure to the level of its neighborhood. Careful judgment of neighborhood values is vital.

■ Is the neighborhood on the upgrade? Check records of real estate transfers and the asking prices in want ads. Do a car window survey to see if other houses in the area are being kept up or whether they are sinking to the level of the clinker you propose to buy.

■ What are zoning regulations? No use building that old wreck into a pretty one-family home only to find that the city planners have just reclassified the block as Z-commercial, available for groceries, bars, or one-room by-the-week rentouts.

■ Can you borrow enough to make the deal pay out? Money is more easily available for financing new structures, particularly for eye-catching condominiums or whole new communities. Lenders aren't always as agreeable to loans on shabby property. You should be able to double the money you put in.

example If you put $4,000.00 down, spend $4,000.00 more—$1,000.00 of your own and $3,000.00 borrowed—and have to endure another $1,000.00 of taxes, insurance, and incidental nicks to the pocketbook, you have put in $6,000.00 altogether. With the value you expect to add to the house, you should be able to get about $12,000.00 over your cost.

When borrowability of the old house won't permit you this kind of leverage, people who know say it's best to forget the project and go seeking another, perhaps more borrowable house.

■ Are the changes basic or surface? New foundations or roofs constitute structural change and cost a lot of money. Things such as paint, moving a wall (sheetrock work does not come high and can be performed with your own hands if you are a weekend carpenter), installing a new appliance or a more modern shower—these are relatively inexpensive surface repairs. Moreover, they add to salability of the house. A new foundation doesn't show and the housewife whose yea or nay will determine her family's decision looks more to her kitchen and to the bathroom than to new roof shingles. Buy where surface changes will do the job. Put on your hat and run if you or the specialist who advises you can see need for basic reconstruction.

If you're out to remodel a street or a block, the rules are different. In its issue of December 15, 1969, *The National Observer* described how three young men, banded together, have done in the "remodel and resell" market. The city was Cincinnati, the section one called Mount Adams:

> Mt. Adams is "a topographically isolated neighborhood," says Neil Bortz, a 35-year-old Harvard Business School graduate who is Towne Properties' president. He moved to Mt. Adams as a bachelor, now lives there with his wife and two small children and is president of the neighborhood association as well. "Whatever tone is set in the dozen-odd streets on the hill can in no way be disturbed or altered by happenings around it. Mt. Adams is indeed an urban island." . . . Neil Bortz's interest in restoration was whetted at Harvard when he took courses under Lewis Mumford, the writer and authority on cities. In 1951 he formed Towne Properties, Inc., with Marvin Rosenberg, 36, a University of Cincinnati law graduate who handles financing, and Lambert

Agin, Jr., 42, a University of Miami graduate who runs Towne's construction branch.

"We bought our first house in Mt. Adams for $6,000," says Marvin Rosenberg. "We were just starting out, Neil was still in school, and it was a big risk for us. But a couple of days after we bought it, a man offered us $12,500 for it. So we sold it, took the $6,500 profit, and plowed it right back into Mt. Adams."

From that modest beginning, Towne's investment in Mt. Adams has grown to where, this fiscal year, it is spending $1,000,000.00 in construction and renovation on Mt. Adams alone. The company also is developing a new office building in downtown Cincinnati, and is involved in a half-dozen large apartment-building projects in Ohio and Kentucky.

Mr. Rosenberg estimates that Towne has remodeled 50 Mt. Adams buildings, sold perhaps 12 others to private renovators, built 50 apartment units, and now owns 60 houses and enough land for 50 more.

In an earlier chapter we stressed that ordinary income was less an objective of inflation fighting than the generation of capital gains. The latter tend to be bigger than ordinary income and have the happy property of being (in most cases) taxed at a lower rate by Uncle Sam's Treasury minions.

Forget that rule when it comes to real estate.

Real estate inflation hedges have the ability (again, in most cases and on specific details you should consult your lawyer, CPA, or other tax adviser) to change ordinary income into capital gains. Far from avoiding income investments in real estate, these can be actively sought.

Real estate investments permit you to take a variety of deductions which are very real in a business sense but which do not reduce the cash flow—the vital, in-the-pocket sums reaching you. It is possible to make a seemingly high income return become almost negligible on the tax return. However, since you have deducted it in great part for depreciation, the writeoff reduces the taxable cost base of a property. You therefore pay a greater capital gains tax upon eventual sale. But you escape the higher tax bite of ordinary income rates. This feature does not apply to raw land, since, unlike buildings or other things which wear out and grind down, land cannot depreciate. Be aware that tax laws change from time to time. (The method you use to calculate depreciation will have a bearing on how much ordinary income can be charged off by depreciation and on whether some of the profit on a sale might become reportable as income. Consult a tax adviser.)

Regarding income generated by real estate, your operative word is *parlay*.

Let the money ride. Reinvest it. Plow it back. That way, high cash flow, taxed only negligibly until sale of a property, can be used to finance more property, which generates still higher tax flow, which permits purchase of still more property. On it goes.

Take a hypothetical case. You have $5,000.00 to invest. With it, you buy income property costing about $50,000.00. You give a $45,000.00 note. Rental income runs about $6,000.00. This finances notes to the mortgage company and leaves around $2,500.00 a year for plowback. Assume you escape taxation because the mortgage interest, upkeep costs, etc., are immediately deductible expenses, and with depreciation of the structure on, say, a fifteen-year table (allowable because the building is not new) you have a small net *loss* for tax purposes which can be used to reduce income taxes on other sources such as your regular job or your business. But you possess the $2,500.00 income which accrues after mortgage costs and running expense even though you escape taxation on it. In two years, you have accumulated another $5,000.00 stake. The depreciation will be used to lessen the taxable cost base of the house, and eventually, if you sell it, you will pay capital gains rates on the amount of profit. With a $5,000.00 stake accumulated from cash flow, you go out looking for a similar house. If successful, you soon have two income producers, and shortly you're searching for a third inflation hedge in the form of income-producing real estate.

(Remember that depreciation rules and changing tax laws govern this chargeoff situation, and in any given case it's wise to have advice of a tax pro.)

Knowledgeable real estaters say that in choosing property

to use as a base for tax-shelter income parlaying, you should consider certain criteria:

1. If parlayed income is the inflation-hedge objective, the more units you have, the merrier the cash registers will tinkle and the more rapidly the cash flow can be added to capital to finance additional units. Avoid single-family structures. Two-family are better. Four-, six-, or ten-family are better still. Go as high in building occupancy as your means and the zoning laws will permit.

2. Be generous with repairs and keep the place modern. Surface work is inexpensive and adds to attractiveness and to the length of time a tenant family will remain.

3. For a modest start, modest rentals are best. That kind of income-producing dwelling will stay rented.

4. Be tough when it comes to payment. The tenant who cannot pay the rent promptly will find it only fractionally easier to pay ten days later. He will find it much harder to pay thirty days later when he owes for two months, and will consider it a positive imposition and injustice if you look for three months' rent at one lick. Donate generously to charity out of your income if you wish. But don't operate an income producer as a charity or you may have no producer of extra dollars for that favorite cause, and no hedge against inflation for the future.

5. In this area, as in real estate purchased primarily for appreciation, the adage that "well bought is half sold" applies. A rule of thumb says gross rentals should come to at least one-tenth of the purchase price each year. Many smart property people look for 12 percent in an inflation-riddled era. Don't "reach" for any piece of property if the price is wrong.

6. Look for neighborhoods on the way up. The area that is sinking into a slum will produce less income next year than it does now, and still less five or ten years hence.

7. Dwellings are preferable to stores for this kind of modest parlayed-income deal. Stores in older areas stay vacant for long periods. The trend is to the shopping center. The center's multiplicity of choices and available customer parking fit the consumer buying patterns of today.

Whether you buy a multi-family dwelling, a big office or apartment building, a downgraded home to remodel in an upbeat section, or raw land, you will have to finance it to enjoy the big leverage advantage of real estate's rapid express. Even in tight-money, high-interest times there are many avenues of financing.

Savings and loan societies are an obvious source of money. Mortgage companies frequently have large sums to dispense as agents for insurance companies and other sizable possessors of capital. Banks make short-term loans for remodeling and repairs. If you are after really big capital to use over a lengthy period of time, local bankers can put you in touch with organizations such as Brooks, Harvey and Co., Inc., of New York, a teamed venture of prestigious Morgan Stanley and Co. and the investment counseling firm of Brooks Harvey. Other Wall Street firms also finance big-block real estate loans.

The seller will often help you to finance a portion—perhaps all—of property you buy from him by taking notes instead of cash.

As the original loan on a piece of property is paid up, you can refinance and use the added capital for new ventures.

example Here is that $50,000.00 multi-family dwelling discussed a few paragraphs back. After a few years you have reduced your indebtedness to $28,000.00 from the original $45,000.00, and as inflation dwindled the dollar during those years, the structure and underlying land came to have an appraised market value of $60,000.00 instead of the $50,000.00 for which you purchased them. Now you have a $32,000.00 equity in the building and the land on which it stands. You should be able to bring your indebtedness up to $48,000.00 or $50,000.00 by refinancing and thus obtain a worthwhile piece of new capital with which to start fresh real estate operations in other property.

SIX QUESTIONS:

Q. *Most ways to finance real estate seem to call for some starting capital. Suppose I don't have this?*

A. Your problem is not unique. Chapter Two looked at some of the methods for raising seed capital. In addition, you can work with the seller to take a second mortgage instead of cash downpayment. Frequently, a seller is anxious to dispose of property for any of a dozen reasons unconnected with its value, and welcomes opportunity to clinch the sale this way.

Q. *Real estate inflation hedging seems conservative. Would I be justified in employing all my basic savings as seed capital?*

A. "All" is a big word. If I were in your shoes, I would not. Before starting on any program to fight inflation, you need to do what a wise military commander would do. Before embarking on a campaign to subdue an enemy army, he would make his base secure. Your base security calls for having enough liquid cash—even though in an inflation era it is dwindling cash—to make sure that if sickness struck or any other unexpected contingency arose, you would not have to hurriedly sell your newly acquired real estate, stocks, bonds, mutual funds, or anything else in order to meet expenses you cannot avoid.

Q. *How would you compare real estate with stocks and mutual funds as an inflation hedge?*

A. About the same way I would compare apples and oranges. I wouldn't try.

Each is an effective hedge. Each has proved to be so in the past and will probably serve well in the years of diminishing currency value which appear to be ahead of us. Each has certain advantages of its own.

With stocks and mutual funds, these advantages include:

■ Liquidity. Securities and mutual fund shares can be bought or sold with a telephone call. Unless you own a sizable block running into millions of dollars (and sometimes even if you do), you can expect that the market will absorb either your offering or your purchase dollars with hardly a tremor. You can be in or out in minutes. Real estate sales or purchases take anything from days (rare) to months to consummate.

■ Low commissions. Security commissions average about 1½ percent. Depending upon the kind of fund it is, a mutual might cost you as much as 8¾ percent if you're buying but in most cases nothing when you want to cash up. Real estate commissions, on the other hand, average out somewhere around 6 percent to buy and another 6 percent to sell.

■ In securities, data on earnings, dividends, price history, etc., are quickly available. You have to dig to get the information about real estate.

Real estate has these advantages:

■ Lack of liquidity is soothing to some inflation hedgers. Long ago, an observer is reputed to have asked the elder J. P. Morgan what the stock market was going to do. "Sir," said Morgan, "it will fluctuate." It has done this ever since. The fluctuations are out in the open, painted across the boardroom tape and printed plain on newspaper pages. In real estate, on the other hand, each piece is individual and its price determinable only on an actual sale. Some people sleep easier without the fluctuations.

■ The investor can add his own values to real estate. He has to wait for the market, the management, and sometimes plain happenstance to add value to his stocks and his mutual funds.

Q. *What do you think of nursing homes as a real estate inflation hedge?*

A. They present difficulties. You have to operate a nursing home. You have to manage it by the minute, day, and week. You have to hire and supervise personnel, comply with many regulations, and do all of this in a specialized field with which few of us are familiar.

Nursing homes were once "Mom and Pop" operations. Typically, a retired registered nurse might run one with her husband helping. Now the field is becoming highly professional. As such it is best left to the pros. If you happen to be one of these pros, however—then go ahead. But keep in mind the toughness of competition you will face from chains and franchised operations.

Q. *In buying and selling real estate, I have to deal with brokers and agents. How ethical are they?*

A. Most are highly so.

However, there is a fringe of shrewd operators and fast-talk specialists. If you take the ordinary precautions you would take in purchasing a car or hiring a plumber—that is, look into the broker's business reputation, how long he has been in operation, whether he has ever been in trouble—then you will probably fare all right.

Q. *Is now a good time to be buying real estate?*

A. I recall the year 1944. The United States was still at war with Japan and I was in the U.S. Naval Reserve. Home on leave, I was astounded to hear from my father that he planned to buy a new home.

"What! Pay $8,500.00 for a house under all that wartime inflation?" I asked. "You must be nuts. Wait till the war is over and prices will simmer down."

No one needs to be told how little prices have simmered down since. Years later I inherited the house and turned down an offer of $50,000.00. My family lives in it today and it would probably bring $60,000.00 if put on the market. Yes, this is a good time to buy real estate.

6
Post Office and Other Games

"I CAN'T BELIEVE all those opportunities in land and property have been in existence for years," commented a friend to whom I read the preceding chapter. "Where was I?"

There are, in addition to the rapid express real estate ideas in Chapter Five, some special real estate operations. He (and you) should know about them.

Be Landlord to Uncle Sam

The following is reprinted, with permission, from a copyrighted article in the *Wall Street Journal,* in the issue of

February 15, 1968, titled, "Buying Post Offices Is Profitable Ploy, Investors Find":

> "Some people collect stamps. I collect post offices." So says Dr. Donald J. Davenport, a Long Beach, California surgeon and one of the kings of the nation's postal landlords. His domain, which he "conservatively" values at $6 million to $7 million, consists of "around 70" U.S. post offices acquired since he first got on the collecting kick about 25 years ago.
>
> "I was tired of standing in line for packages," he says, "so I asked the fellow why they didn't build a bigger building. He said, 'Why don't you?' and I said I couldn't, it was the Government's. He said I could—so I did."
>
> Dr. Davenport isn't the only one who did. Of the 29,662 buildings occupied by the Post Office Department at the end of last June, 26,715 . . . were privately owned and leased to the Government. Expanding mail volume and a shifting population are adding to the demand for new space, and, though some Congressional economizers grumble that it's costing the Government extra, a parade of affluent investors are discovering the financial benefits of post office ownership.

Since competitive bidding is the rule for awarding leases, the return is not always tremendous. But it is always adequate, and the appeal of being landlord to Uncle Sam does not lie in the ordinary rental income such a setup generates. The big appeal is in the buildup of capital so that an inflation-hedging asset is gradually developed at no risk.

Consider:

- You build, then rent the building.
- You are able to build on extremely low downpayment, so that maximum leverage exists. A lease with the government is gilt-edged collateral. Postal landlords say that the amount needed to swing one of these construction contracts is only a fraction of normal. One such landlord estimated required starting capital at one-third the capital required for other large buildings. (However, such capital is not always small by absolute size, for when you put up a sizable struc-

ture you are dealing with dollar amounts that might swing an apartment building or shopping center.)

■ You amortize the cost over the period of the rental lease.

■ Leases often specify that if local property taxes go up, the rental will be increased to cover this.

■ At the end of the lease you should have an existing capital asset worth anywhere from a few hundred thousand dollars to several million, which you can then sell, re-lease, or use as you please—an inflation hedge.

How to get into this is explained in a brochure, *The Post Office Leasing Program.* It points out:

> Privately owned buildings include post offices of all sizes as well as garages, general office quarters, and specialized installations required to move today's mail. Mail volume is increasing so rapidly that more than 5,000 new post offices will be needed in the next five years.
>
> When a post office becomes crowded, the Department begins a study to determine the building area. Mail volume, transportation, population growth, carrier routes and other matters are considered. Site availability is studied and plans and specifications are determined.
>
> When a small post office is needed in a rural or suburban community, the Regional Real Estate Office will advertise for bids on the basis of standard plans and specifications for construction and lease of a building. The bidder provides the site. A contract is awarded to the responsible bidder whose bid is most advantageous to the government. When the building is completed and accepted by the Post Office Department, rental payments are authorized. Title to the property remains with the bidder.
>
> Standard plans and specifications cannot be used for a larger building. In this case, the Regional Real Estate Office usually obtains options on several suitable sites. When the final selection has been made, the other options are released and the Department prepares plans for the building. All bidders then can base their bids upon the known land cost and building construction requirements.
>
> Interested persons or firms who wish to be placed on the bidder's mailing list for postal projects should contact the Regional Real Estate Office serving the area in which there is an

interest. Invitations to bid are issued by the Regional Office for each project in that region. Notices of bid solicitations are given to news media and are posted in the local post offices. To be placed on the bidder's list for major facilities, those which will exceed 50,000 square feet net interior, interested persons should contact the Director, Realty Division, Bureau of Facilities, Post Office Department, Washington, D.C. 20260.

Prospective bidders for specific projects are upon request furnished packages containing instructions, contract forms, plans and construction requirements and other bidding details. On a major facility project, the Department enters into an agreement for architect and engineering services with a local firm and the bid package will include complete working plans and detailed specifications. In these instances, the bidder must pay the cost of the plans and specifications. The successful bidder will reimburse the Department or the architect and engineering firm for fees under the contract.

Contracts are awarded to the lowest responsible bidder providing the most attractive annual rental for the basic lease term. The Department reserves the right after bid opening to negotiate with the low bidder on all rental rates or other terms and conditions of the bid, without waiving its right to accept the bid as submitted. The Department may also reject any or all bids. When net interior space amounts to 3,000 square feet or more, bid bonds are required. The successful bidder must provide a performance bond and a labor and material payment bond when required under the terms of the accepted agreement.

Lease terms of ten years are most frequent, but leases for 20 or 30 years are entered into for larger facilities. In some cases, regardless of the length of the basic term, options for renewal are provided. In some instances, options to purchase are included. The leases usually provide for building maintenance to be the landlord's responsibility. General housekeeping and janitorial services are the responsibility of the government. For many of the leased facilities, tax clause riders are included whereby the government agrees to pay all general real estate taxes levied on the leased premises.

Nothing in life is foolproof, even when you play post office. Certain cautions must be exercised. One of these is to see that the lease period and the loan period coincide where possible.

That way, your payoff on the structure comes with expiration of its use by the government. Afterward there is excellent chance that a lease may be renewed. If not, however, you are clear financially.

Another caution involves the fact that, even in a day of high-yield money, your rental income may be small in relation to rents on other property. Bidding is usually heated and as a result you can't count upon winning one of these leases. But you won't incur any risk or liability unless you do.

If present proposals to convert the Post Office into a semi-private corporation go through, this setup may—or may not —be subject to later change.

The Arithmetic of Resorts

Between Bay St. Louis and the Bay of Biloxi stretches the lush Gulf Coast of Mississippi, a resort area its residents like to call America's Riviera. Part spills west of the bay in the communities of Bay St. Louis, Waveland, and Clermont Harbor. Over a four-lane bridge at Bay St. Louis moves the resort-bound traffic from New Orleans. There three years ago I stood with a friend.

"This is the crossroads," we agreed. "Here is the place for a public swimming pool and amusement area." Our vision of an inflation hedge extraordinary might have been fulfilled if Hurricane Camille, the worst natural disaster ever to strike the continental United States, had not wiped the Gulf Coast of dwellings, stores, and trees and even removed the sand of the beach itself in August 1969. Because this was the kind of offbeat, special opportunity that can be created in resort real estate, it is interesting to review the arithmetic which convinced us of a hedge opportunity at that spot.

Our North American society is able to produce all of its needs in only a fraction of its working time. As a result most of us have more money to jingle in our pockets. And we work fewer hours to get it. Put these facts together and they spell l-e-i-s-u-r-e. Leisure with money to enjoy it. That is why resort land and other real estate have gone up tremendously in price during the past decade. Because the trend is expected to continue and even accelerate, the worth of resorts as inflation hedges should increase.

We estimated the cost of a swimming and amusement area at $200,000.00 but did not need to raise the sum until we had secured control over land beside the bay bridge where east-west traffic funneled. From either side of the bay, a short ride made the location available to dwellers and vacationers in six communities.

The asking price was $35,000.00. The land stretched 250 yards back from beachfront. With an available loan, it could have been handled for $5,000.00 downpayment and closing costs. The operation was to be incorporated and stock representing 45 percent ownership sold to the public. We felt this would raise the necessary operating funds to begin construction of the pool, using an additional loan to complete it.

Across the grass plot between road and beach, a putt-putt course would be constructed. Later, if need arose or opportunity offered, a driving range might be built on adjoining land.

For active management of the operation, we would be paid in warrants to buy stock rather than in cash, giving a tax-saving angle and providing the ability to build up a capital asset at moderate cost.

In its Technical Bulletin called *Planning and Developing Waterfront Property* (copyright 1964), the authoritative Urban Land Institute noted:

> Waterfront real estate is such a relatively limited commodity that when it is not adversely affected by industry or the elements it commands premium prices. When the waterfront is on usable, quiet water suitable for boating, this premium is further enhanced. It is not unusual to find a value ratio between lots just off the water and lots on the water as great as four to one.

The same bulletin described imaginative use of existing

facilities whose resort potential had been unrealized at Lake San Marcos in northern San Diego County, California:

> The developers, Frazar Brothers, Inc., experienced California builders, realized the potential value and advantages of an existing, unkempt reservoir in an area where privately owned lakes are practically non-existent. Around this center, they are creating as attractive a community as can be found in the booming Southern California region. . . .
>
> The sales and price pattern at Lake San Marcos is a vivid illustration of the influence of the waterfront on real estate values.
>
> Prior to the start of Lake San Marcos, the area had had only spotty development, and, while there had been speculative increases on land prices, there was generally a depressed market for homes and lots. $5,000.00 was and still is a high price for a 6,000–7,000-square-foot lot outside Lake San Marcos.
>
> Within Lake San Marcos, a successful sales program has been achieved within the following price ranges:
>
> Single family homes (1,200 to 1,600 s.f.) on 60′–70′ wide lakefront lots—$40,000 to $45,000.
>
> Duplex units (1,000 to 1,500 s.f.) on 30′ x 133′ lakefront lots—$34,000–$50,000.
>
> Condominium units next to the lake (800 to 1,000 s.f.)—$18,000–$25,000.
>
> Fairway homes (1,200 to 1,600 s.f.) on 60′–70′ wide lots—$29,000–$35,000.

Whether you plan to use resort land on a grand scale as was done at Lake San Marcos—remembering that leveragability of land reduces the amount of capital needed for such a project —or to buy up some beachfront as hedge against eroding dollars, you must be aware of certain cautions inherent in this kind of operation. Hurricane Camille, which erased so much of the Mississippi Gulf Coast from Clermont Harbor to Biloxi, is an example. Because such forces can break out at any time, insurance rates are high. Some insurance protections are unobtainable at any price.

Resort real estate is not as salable as is property in more

built-up areas. If you want to unload urban property and things are slow at the moment, it might take six months to get what you consider a right price. It could take that long when things are good in a resort area, and perhaps two years in slower times.

Ride the Boating Boom

In its issue of July 19, 1969, *Business Week* reported on what it termed the "Good Life Afloat":

> A ten-minute ride in a taxi takes Richard Roberts, a New York stockbroker, to his second home. It's a 46-foot Chris Craft houseboat moored at a Hudson River marina, a cab hop away from his Fifth Ave. apartment overlooking Central Park. The Roberts houseboat lists at $30,000.00, but it ran over $40,000.00 with such extras as air conditioning, heat, independent power supply, and ship-to-shore telephone.
>
> Roberts is one of a growing army of houseboat buyers who are discovering the joy of waterfront living. Old salts sneer at them, some marinas won't take them, but houseboats are beginning to cluster in colonies along the nation's waterways.

New York City would hardly be classified as a resort area, and Mr. Roberts' maritime way of living points up the fact that you can ride the boating boom anywhere. Land available for marinas or occasional boat usage can soar in value as inflation eats at the dollar over the years. In its study on waterfront property the Urban Land Institute commented on this fast market. The figures dated back several years. To update them, it would be necessary to add zeros, since boat usage is more widespread now than ever before and promises to continue growing:

> The general boating market is much greater than that portion of it which influences marinas and urban waterfront properties [noted the study]. A few statistics will give a measure of the vast appeal boats and boating have for the American public. Here

is obviously an attraction that has yet to be fully realized by community builders.

1963 was a good year for boats. According to the magazine *The Boating Industry,* 38,390,000 persons used the waterways of the nation more than twice. For this pleasure, they spent $2.58 billion. Not counting rafts and inner tubes, they were carried on 7,678,000 recreation boats, divided among 813,000 inboard powered (including auxiliary sail), 495,000 sailboats, 4,239,000 outboard boats, and 2,131,000 rowboats, canoes and lesser craft.

Those who spurned the wind, or their own muscle, powered 949,000 inboard and 6,390,000 outboard engines with 535,-000,000 gallons of gas. Of this inboard engines consumed more than their share of strength by swallowing 160 million gallons vs. 375 million gallons for outboards. . . . Generally speaking, more people spend more money on more boats and more powerful engines each year. Water safety has been improving even as the waters become more crowded.

While outboard power dominates the boating field, the *Wall Street Journal* has pointed out that sailboard retail volume in 1963 was $25 million, an increase of 66 per cent over 1961, compared with an overall increase in boating spending of 3 per cent.

Even without standing such numbers on end or comparing them with the national debt, they are impressive.

One conclusion is obvious. The greatest use of boats is in those which can be trailered, not in the glamorous, over-$10,000 market.

Whether you can opt for building and operating a vast, well-accoutered, full-service marina or merely build a boat landing, you should check availability of roads. You cannot expect boat owners to bring trailered vessels up to the shores of Lake Swamp Water unless your area is close to a good highway.

And ask how many boat owners live within trailering distance. If yours is a desert area of the West, even a usable body of water won't guarantee success if the county population consists of eighteen persons, three of whom are old ladies and twelve are children. Build where a market exists.

Then check out competition. If there are 183 boat owners

within trailering distance, and 182 marinas exist to serve them, appreciation prospects for the 183rd marina are slim.

FIVE QUESTIONS:

Q. *The things you mention require borrowing. At today's interest rates that costs a lot. What are the possibilities of mortgage money?*

A. Possibilities are there. Perhaps you can arrange, as many do, to borrow at relatively low interest and lend out at high interest. It is a good way to make money. *But—*

Think before you do it. Are you hedging against inflation, or just going into the mortgage business? Keep in mind that two of the requisites for beating inflation are to put capital into things rather than money, and to avoid as much as possible high taxation at ordinary income rates.

By doing the mortgage bit you negate both of these rules. Your capital will be in money. Your taxation will be high because interest received is ordinary income.

example   You are able to borrow money at 8 percent and can lend it out on a first or second mortgage at 16 percent. Your "profit" is 8 percent, leaving out the drag of overhead which would be there in actual operation.

But inflation is going on at 7 percent a year, a pace it has frequently achieved and at which it was moving when 1969 came to its unlamented close. Your real gain has been whittled to a meager 1 percent (8 percent interest less 7 percent inflation depreciation of the dollar). Then the tax collector comes along and notes that you are in a 35 percent tax bracket. He says, "Okay, you have a reportable profit of 8 percent. At your tax rate, I want 2.8 percent of your take." So you keep only 5.2 percent. Inflation whittles away 7 percent and you remain with an actual, accountable *loss* of 1.8 percent. That is a poor way to "beat" inflation.

Q. *How do I find out about Post Office expansion plans?*

A. Contact your Regional Post Office. These offices are in the

John Hancock Bldg., Atlanta, Ga. 30304, serving Florida, Georgia, North Carolina, and South Carolina; Post Office and Courthouse Bldg., Boston, Mass. 02109, serving Connecticut, Maine, Massachusetts, New Hampshire, Rhode Island, and Vermont; Main Post Office Bldg., Chicago, Ill. 60699, serving Illinois and Michigan; c/o P.O. Box 1999 in Cincinnati, Ohio 45201, for Indiana, Kentucky, and Ohio; Box 3, Main Post Office, Dallas, Tex. 75221 for Louisiana and Texas; P.O. Box 1979, Denver, Colo. 80201 for Arizona, Colorado, New Mexico, Utah, and Wyoming; Post Office Bldg., Memphis, Tenn. 38101 for Alabama, Mississippi, and Tennessee; Federal Bldg., Minneapolis, Minn. 55425, serving Minnesota, North Dakota, South Dakota, and Wisconsin; Main Post Office Bldg., New York, N.Y. 10098, serving New York, Puerto Rico, and the Virgin Islands; General Post Office, Philadelphia, Pa. 19104, serving Delaware, New Jersey, and Pennsylvania; 1114 Market St., St. Louis, Mo. 63199, for Arkansas, Iowa, and Missouri; 631 Howard St., San Francisco, Calif. 94106, for California, Hawaii, and Nevada; P.O. Box 9000, Seattle, Wash. 98109, serving Alaska, Idaho, Montana, Oregon, and Washington; 521 Twelfth St., N.W., Washington, D.C. 20269, serving the District of Columbia, Maryland, Virginia, and West Virginia; and Main Post Office Bldg., Wichita, Kans. 67200, for Kansas, Nebraska, and Oklahoma.

Q. *Aren't desirable water sites about gone?*

A. People probably said that back in George Washington's day when all of Virginia had been settled and pioneers had to filter across the mountains into the back beyond to find land. No, the sites aren't all gone. Somebody saw the potential at Lake San Marcos, California, when that now-booming water site was bedraggled and unwanted. If you have vision and imagination, there are many Lake San Marcos situations around.

Q. *Landing areas for houseboats look interesting. Would this apply only in coastal areas?*

A. Houseboating is most popular on the seacoasts and around big lakes. But it is catching on elsewhere. In the northern part of my state, the biggest stream running through a town of 80,000 is a bayou 100 feet across at its widest and less than that throughout most of its length. There are fifty people in that small community who own houseboats and who cruise down the winding bayou to a small lake 50 miles distant.

At one inland community, almost 200 houseboats are docked, and similar activities are growing everywhere. A large national organization recently started a floating hotel system of stationary houseboats.

Q. *Do real estate syndicates offer inflation-hedging opportunities?*

A. In the right kind of setup—yes. But you don't get the full inflation hedge, since the syndicate managers understandably want their cut of success. Where a syndicate is well run by experienced hands and shows good results, you can escape management worries and still benefit.

If a deal of your own goes bad, you can back out by selling and starting again. But bits and pieces of a syndicate are not always easy to sell if you want out.

7

Everyman's Oil Well

"MA, WE DONE HIT. The well is a-flowin' and Pa says we gonna be rich." Those words have figured in countless movies about the sudden-wealth dreams of Americans. Most of us tend to sum up financial hope in a wistful statement: "Maybe I'll hit oil this year."

Until recently, the reality of that dream was confined to a handful of wildly successful wildcatters. Most of us don't know how to go about oil drilling and exploration, can't tell oil sands from roof slates, and haven't the money or the will power to go into oil exploration anyway.

Now anyone with a stake as small as $1,500.00 and a hankering for the old American oil dream can indulge that hankering. No matter that he knows nothing about oil and barely differentiates the stuff that goes into his car's gas tank from the stuff that lubricates his wheels. Experts stand ready to serve the inflation hedger with a stake of that thousand and a half. Moreover, while its inflation hedge functions best for well-oiled investors of wealth, the attraction of oil is now possible for all who want to try petroleum participations as a means to, possibly, beat inflation's ravages.

What They Are

The first thing to understand about participation partnerships is that they are b-i-g. Although investors can get into some (not all) of them with amounts as small as a $1,500.00 stake, the total value of the petroleum participations taken together is well over $1 billion. More than 100 partnerships swing this sizable sum. There is nothing new, untried, or untested about the idea. But there is nothing guaranteed about it, either. It is important to understand that there is no more warranty of success, profit, and inflation hedge about the participations than there is to any other effort in the fight against dwindling dollars.

You should not confuse petroleum participations offered to the public with old-time wildcatting, although some verge upon that kind of activity. Texas Tom and his wildcat drill are largely a thing of the past in this day when it takes over a million dollars to put down the average hole, and a driller has less than an even chance that the hole will hit anything except sand and dust. Texas Tom is found more often on the pages of a nostalgic book or a roaring late-movie adventure-from-yesterday than on the high plains of the Texas Panhandle or the swampy lowlands of Louisiana. In his best day, Tex couldn't afford to put down an offshore hole; the people you see out on deepwater rigs are a far cry from a movie wildcatter.

Increasingly, people on the rigs, in the dry West Texas plains, or the wet South Louisiana swamps work for well-heeled partnerships of the kind this chapter is about. If you buy into an oil participation deal, they work for you.

The big oil play of 1969 was the North Slope of Alaska. It took millions to bid on explorations rights. The oil industry's big boys were represented when bids were opened. But all of the acreage was not bid in by them. A sizable portion went to participation partnerships whose investors—some putting up sums as small as that $1,500.00 minimum participation accepted by a few partnerships—thus found themselves Alaskan oil operators able to boast to friends about personal stakes on the fabled North Slope of America's newest Golconda Land.

"It is not like owning some common stock in one of the successful bidders," one happy partner told me after the bidding concluded. "My stake is personal. It's oil, not just a stock certificate evidencing tenuous ownership of a firm so vast that I'm lost on its stockholder rolls."

Where else such a feeling but in oil partnerships? Where else such an inflation hedge as Everyman's Oil Well?

Here's how the *California Financial Journal* explained the lure of oil programs in a front-page article in its November 18, 1969 issue:

> Drilling programs are designed to mutually benefit an oil company and a group of high tax bracket investors. The company has the skills to find oil but lacks the necessary capital to finance drilling operations. The investors seek a means to reduce current tax liability and an investment that offers potential for high returns.
>
> Investors supply capital by purchasing "units" in a drilling program. With the proceeds, the oil company buys leases, conducts geological investigations and drills a series of wells. Income from successful wells is shared according to a predetermined formula. Because oil companies constantly need funds to drill for new oil, and because increased affluence has made the American taxpayer aware of the benefits of tax-sheltered investments, drilling programs have grown rapidly.

Robert G. Mount, President of Charter Street Corp., distributor for GeoTek Resources Fund of San Francisco, points out four advantages of the petroleum participation:

> 1) Tax Shelter. It is anticipated that more than 70% of your investment may be deductible against your own ordinary income in the year drilling operations are completed.

2) Diversification. Your investment will be spread among many drilling prospects. These prospects will include drilling on proven and semi-proven acreage and also on exploratory acreage, where new reserves of oil and gas offering high profit potential are the motivating factor.

3) Non-assessable. No additional investment is required in the . . . program.

4) Limited Liability. The participant becomes a limited partner in the drilling operation.

In more detail, the prospectus of Clinton Oil Co. explains the operation of participation programs:

> The company has conducted annual oil and gas programs since 1963, funds for which are provided through sales to the public by the company of participating interests in the programs. The company fully manages the programs and expenditure of funds thereof. The purpose of the programs is to engage in oil and gas exploration and the acquisition of producing properties.
>
> Under terms of the Program Agreements, participants in the program pay 75 percent and the company 25 percent of the acquisition and exploration (venture) fund. The company receives 10 percent of the venture fund as an overhead fee. For their respective interests the participants and the company each receive a 50 percent working interest in each program. A unit of participation is $10,000 of which $7,000 is paid to an account for acquisition and exploration of properties and drilling, completion and equipping of the first productive well by the company, if any, on leases; $2,400 is paid to an account to be applied pursuant to the provisions of the Operating Agreement to the extent needed for equipping, developing and operating expenses of properties on which productive wells, if any, may be completed; and $600 is paid as a sales commission. Operating costs are borne by the participants and the company in direct proportion to their respective ownerships in the property.

(As you can see in this long paragraph, the company receives 10 percent off the top. It puts up 25 percent of the acquisition and exploration costs. It then has 50 percent working interest. The setup of each fund is different, and it pays to be sure of what you're receiving before covering the bottom line with your signature and your signature with a check.)

An unusual setup is that of California Time Petroleum, Inc. Thomas L. North, editor and publisher of *North's News Letter and Special Reports,* pointed out in a letter to his clients that in California Time's reversionary interest plan,

> . . . the participants will bear all costs of acquiring the properties and all costs of drilling, completion, operation or abandonment of each well drilled including overhead expenses allocable to the 1969 fund, and participants will receive all income from the program's interest in *all* wells in the program until they receive payout of all such costs, including management and administrative fees. After payout, the participants are to receive 75% of production income, and California Time 25%. It appears that most exploratory programs call for payout on a lease block basis rather than an overall program basis.

North further explained the diversification of a typical participation operation:

> The 1969 program is weighted to give a well balanced exposure to various types of risk. After reviewing 75 to 100 exploratory plays, 16 were selected as having sufficient merit and potential size in the wildcat category, or an equivalent of 8 net wells, using 20% of the available fund (assumed at maximum). Close-in or development type drilling will absorb 60% of the fund, for 20 planned wells (10 net). The remaining 20% of the fund would be used to purchase approximately 30 producing wells on a basis of 1/3 cash, and 2/3rds in reserved production payments. Geographical balance is also planned, with 20% of efforts directed to the California area, 20% to the Rocky Mountain area, 20% to Canada, 30% to the Mid-Continent, and 10% to the Gulf Coast.

The Big Tax Break

Let an expert tell it like it is. Writing in the January 20, 1970 issue of *California Financial Journal,* John H. Jonk, CPA, of the Beverly Hills office of Price Waterhouse and Co., noted:

> Individuals who invest in oil and gas properties through oil participation funds immediately recoup the majority of the in-

vestment through tax savings, if they are in a high tax bracket.

Contrary to many other investments, where the tax benefits of the dollars invested are deferred to the future or are spread over a period of years, participants in oil and gas funds obtain their tax benefits currently. This occurs because the portion of the money invested by the participants that is expended on intangible drilling and development costs can be deducted for income tax purposes.

Intangible drilling and development costs include labor, fuel, repairs, hauling and supplies used in the drilling of wells and other activities necessary for the preparation of wells for the production of oil or gas. These costs are considered to have no salvage value even though incurred in connection with the installation of physical property which has a salvage value.

However, amounts paid for materials used to construct the physical structures are not included. In most oil participation funds, 70 to 90 percent of the money received from the investor is immediately spent on or allocated to intangible costs. If this occurs, the investor receives a significant tax benefit in the same year that he parts with his money. And, this advantage will not be altered by the Tax Reform Act of 1969 recently signed into law by the President.

If the fund discovers oil or gas, the income from the sale of oil or gas is partially tax-free to the investor. Under the prior law, $27\frac{1}{2}$ percent of the gross income before production expenses and taxes was allowed as a deduction for depletion. The Tax Reform Act reduced the $27\frac{1}{2}$ percent rate to 22 percent. This deduction is limited (as was the case under prior law) to 50 percent of the net income from each oil or gas property. Also, as a result of the change in the tax law, part or all of the percentage depletion claimed by the investor could be subject to a minimum tax of 10 percent. This tax would be levied in addition to the normal income tax paid by the taxpayer. . . .

Some oil participation funds use leverage to enhance the return to the investor. This is usually done by borrowing money for developing properties where oil or gas has been located. If the transaction is properly structured, the investor may have allocated to him cumulative tax losses during the development stage that exceed his total investment.

Even if the fund is totally unsuccessful, the loss to the investor is reduced. He is entitled to an ordinary deduction for the portion of the original investment which was not claimed as a deduction for intangible drilling and development costs.

On the other hand, the investor is entitled to long-term capital gain treatment on part or all of any gain on the sale of his interest in oil or gas properties (or his interest in an oil participation fund), provided he has owned the investment for over six months. The investor will realize ordinary income to the extent the sales proceeds represent a recovery of depreciation on tangible equipment. Normally this represents a small portion of the total sales proceeds.

Many of the tax benefits obviously apply to an inflation hedger who is in high tax brackets. For most of the rest of us, the participations offer a different hedge—investment in common stocks of the companies that run these participations. Many enjoy tax advantages, and earnings are favorably affected by lower taxes. Speaking, hopefully, a stock's price should be levered higher by this tax hedge.

How Participations Fight Inflation

The first thing you see in petroleum participations is their tax shelter. But these possess another advantage: the ability to gradually build into capital assets over the years.

In real estate, tax laws permit conversion of some current income into capital. It is that way in petroleum participations. "Heck, I have the money," one investor told me. "But if I still have it in the form of ordinary income by the end of this year, I am sure to lose a lot of it to the Treasury's tax boys. So I employ the petroleum play to let me turn my own income into capital that, at the end of the program and if the program goes well, I can own. The participation generally qualifies as a capital asset when I get out. If I sell it, I am taxed at long-term capital gains rates. If I keep the income I have now instead of going into this sort of deal, I will be taxed at ordinary income rates, and my ability to build up capital as a counter to inflation losses will be severely limited."

There are great plowback possibilities in petroleum. One of the largest participation operations is run by King Resources Co. Writing in the May 6, 1969 issue of *California Financial Journal,* John M. King, then chairman of King Resources, noted:

> Perhaps I can best explain . . . by taking the investment dollar through its course. An investor buys a limited partnership in any given quarter. When an oil company receives the money, they acquire leases and get the men and equipment to drill as many wells as possible with the money available. *Money netted from the production of successful wells is reinvested in subsequent quarterly partnerships. The key to economic success is reinvestment.* [Italics are the author's.]

Mr. King believes there always will be new participations in which to plow back the tax-sheltered profits.

> The demand for petroleum products is increasing faster than our industry has been able to meet that demand," he wrote. "The Department of the Interior is currently projecting a demand of 80 billion barrels of crude oil and natural gas liquids between now and 1980. The demand for natural gas during this same . . . period is expected to reach the astronomical figure of 310 trillion cubic feet.
>
> To meet such demands, the United States must produce as much oil and gas in the next eleven years as it produced in the last 111 years, or since the day in 1859 when Col. Drake drilled the nation's first successful oil well.

Avoid These Dangers

Do you recall the initial enthusiasm for hedge funds? Such funds sold some stocks short and purchased others long. The idea was to always have shorts on the weakest stocks and to own the strongest stocks. Thus no matter the market climate, hedge fund theory held, you would be protected against sudden shifts of direction and should make a lot of money. Hedge fund partners generally did make money and new hedge funds sprang up every week. Some went public by becoming mutual funds. Bright young men of Wall Street, fresh from

Harvard Business School and certain that they and their computers couldn't miss, moved into the new approach.

Then came the 1969 bear market. The hedge idea should have functioned brilliantly. But it didn't. Two of the poorest performers among mutual funds in that year of shrinking stock values were publicly held hedge funds. The year 1969 showed that the ability of shrewd, knowledgeable hedge analysts was a more important factor in hedge fund success than the concept itself.

Today, some enthusiasts say that petroleum participations can't miss. "Why, with all that tax shelter, how can anyone lose? You are only putting up 50-cent dollars, anyway," enthuse the bright new men.

It is probable that in this field, as in operating a hedge fund, the abilities of operating firms will count for a great deal more in the long run than the participation concept itself. Carried out by able operators, participations are likely to do well. In inept hands they may fail.

■ Nonliquidity is another danger of oil participations. No ready market is there if you have to sell to meet an emergency, send Jimmie to an expensive university, or cash up because you'd like to count your one-dollar bills by spreading them out on the floor and walking over the lovely green stuff.

■ Some participation management companies try to maintain (but don't guarantee to do so) a market for those who want to sell. Under such a setup you may get as much as it is worth or you may not. One management firm assesses a penalty fee on those who withdraw in less than a stated number of years or for other than a very few reasons it considers permissible.

■ Sometimes management remuneration double-dips. Many take a fee plus a slice of the action, with no investment to back up that slice. Investors are penalized by having a partner whose withdrawal of a share of profits and income is not matched with a risk of his capital. "I don't mind paying one fee," said a knowledgeable financier with whom I discussed this. "But not all participation plans give a fair break in this direction. Of course, I am expressing a personal view of the situation and not making an indictment of anybody."

■ Those not in high tax brackets should know that the principal attraction of the participation is its ability to shelter investments from taxes, thus creating what one observer termed the "marvelous metamorphosis of income into capital." In real estate and other types of inflation hedge it is possible to employ borrowed money so that with a smaller stake you can work big projects. In the stock market the small investor can use leverage such as Puts and Calls, margin, and warrant options to make his limited capital do big things. No leverage is available here.

SIX QUESTIONS:

Q. *Can I buy a program participation with a major oil company such as Standard Oil (N.J.) or Texaco?*

A. No. The majors have tremendous cash flow from their world-wide operations and don't seek money to explore or exploit a field.

However, some companies that sell public participations are far from small. One approaches half a billion dollars—hardly jingling change even in the leagues where Standard Oil (N.J.) and Texaco play oil ball.

So you can count on being in the bigger leagues with the companies that do give out participations. And in most cases you have working for you the same quality of geological, engineering, legal, and other talent that the Jerseys and Texacos employ.

None of that will guarantee success, of course. Even the majors don't hit on every hole. Or on every sixth or seventh hole, either. And the odds are even longer offshore than on land. Many participation companies try to cut down those odds by drilling in proven or semi-proven areas.

Q. *How do I buy petroleum participations?*

A. Most stock and bond brokerage houses sell them. Commissions range up to about 8 percent, much higher than on ordinary securities transactions and about in line with loading charges assessed on front-end load mutual funds. Some brokerage firms offer wide participation selections just as they offer mutual fund selections, and a number give specialized advice.

Q. *Is there the equivalent of a no-load mutual fund in which I don't have to pay big starting commissions to get aboard?*

A. Yes. There are programs that charge no fee to get in. But most charge a fee. As is the case with mutual funds, the existence or absence of a loading charge-type commission should not be your sole—or even your main—criterion in picking a petroleum program. Rather, study such factors as these nine questions suggested by Robert L. James of Marschalk Co., Inc.:

1. Does the program provide that the investor get back 100 percent of his invested dollars before the operator receives his interest or his net profit interest?

2. Are the prospects to be drilled in known oil areas or are they straight wildcats?

3. Does the operator assure adequate geophysical and geological study to support and warrant projected drilling expenses?

4. Does the operator propose to drill only when the leases to be included in the program cover adequate acreage so that in the event of a discovery development wells can be drilled?

5. Does the operator intend to drill below 1,200 feet at which point drilling costs geometrically increase because of higher pressures and temperature and other technical factors?

6. Does the operator intend to drill only in areas where there are multiple pay zone horizons so that the investor is getting more than one shot for his money?

7. Has the program been designed and structured so that, if successful, the projects to be included in the program will return the investors' money back over a four- or five-year period of time?

8. Is there a ready market for the oil and gas that might be discovered in the program? It is of little value to the individual investor seeking income or a return on his money to participate

in a program where successful wells are shut off because they cannot be hooked up to a pipeline.

9. What is the program's risk ratio to reward factor? What are the qualitative and quantitative risk factors? Is there a product mix in the program so that the investor can diversify his investment into a reasonable spread between development drilling, semi-proved drilling and wildcatting?

Q. *Do program operators carry out all actual drilling?*

A. Some do, others don't. With one firm, all drilling is done by a subsidiary. Other firms contract (occasionally with the big oil companies) to develop a field. Some call for competitive bids on each new program. No way is better than the others; it is the skill of a whole team that counts, along with the kind of acreage being developed.

Q. *Are there governmental regulations for investors' protection?*

A. Most programs register with the Securities and Exchange Commission. Recently, the SEC issued uniform guidelines for these statements, and proposals have been offered to make the participation programs come under the regulative umbrella of the Investment Company Act that empowers SEC supervision of mutual funds.

Q. *How long has this kind of participating activity been going on?*

A. One company traces its activity in public participation in petroleum ventures back to 1954. Most of the industry is new, however.

8

A Farm to Fight Inflation

YEARS AGO, one of my father's friends retired. He had been vice-president of a medium-sized corporation. "Yep," he told us, "me for the easy life. I'm going to move out beyond the suburbs and become a gentleman farmer. Probably make a lot of money at it, too, when I apply business methods to farming."

The term "gentleman farm" was much in use in those days, which were also times of stable currency and prices you could count upon. Without saying so, it contained a lofty premise that when city-slicker methods were put into the soil along with the manure and compost from last year's crop residue—chemical fertilizers weren't much in use as yet—then things would really hum.

They hummed for my father's old friend. Two years later I

saw him on the street, dressed as neatly as ever, and I asked whether he had indeed found a way to put such efficiency into farming that the raising of crops and animals was now done without disturbing the sharpness of his trouser crease or the exact windsor knot in his necktie.

"To tell you the truth," he answered, "I'm not farming any more. Moved back to the city. I can't understand how every farmer isn't broke. Why, eggs alone cost so much that I figure they'd have to sell at $5.00 each in order to break me even."

Farming has changed since that day. One thing that probably isn't greatly different, however, is the fact that retired corporation vice-presidents are no better fitted to farm profitably than my father's old crony was. *Unless—*

Unless, that is, they go about farming the financially modern way. Then a farm can indeed become a mighty engine for fighting inflation. And the beauty is that you, I, or my father's friend need have no more knowledge than the pitifully small store of agricultural wisdom with which a successful vice-president once thought himself equipped to succeed along the rural roads as he had amid the city's concrete.

In those days, successful vice-presidents, unless they had been vice-presidents of oil and oil-oriented corporations, weren't very likely to succeed in the business of finding, refining, or marketing petroleum products, either. Along came the modern concept of a petroleum participation, described in the previous chapter. Under this concept people who know nothing about petroleum become limited partners and people who do know oil and its intricacies become general partners who manage affairs so the whole rancho of participations will (it is hoped) make money.

Now you can apply the concept to farming, with an eye to making the old "gentleman farm" of my father's friend's day into a tool for combating inflation and maybe piling up your income and capital values faster than the dollar can erode.

Cattle raising, citrus groves, and a new thing called "catfish farming" are in the big time. Wall Street has joined the act. With Wall Street's entry comes opportunity to "institutionalize" farming for you and me. Before you go too deeply into this, however, you should understand that *the biggest benefit is in tax savings. The principal appeal is therefore to people in high tax brackets.*

Cattle

Hoot Gibson and Tom Mix wouldn't recognize cattle farming as it is done today. Neither would the later generation of cowboy heroes such as Hopalong Cassidy or Roy Rogers who cavorted on television. It is a *business* now, as organized, but-toned down, regimented, cost-accounted, and mass production-minded as any in Detroit or Gary.

Here's the spread. Old J. J., trail boss, grizzled and two-gunned, is riding along into the sunset. Beside him rides his pard, A. A., assistant grizzled, two-gunned trail boss.

"This big ranch ain't the same, A. A.," says J. J. with a flip of one gun. "Why, when you and me broke in as young cow-hands on the Rio Grande, the boss was K. K., who killed three men before he was twenty and died with his guns a-blazin' before he was thirty, taking eighteen of them no-good coyotes from the Circle Bad Guys along with him to the cowhand's big ranch up there in the sky."

"Nope, J. J., t'ain't what she uster be," agreed A. A., shifting a terbaccy quid to the other side of a mouth grown straight with loneliness on the Western range and squinting up at the sky with eyes puckered from squinting too long at the sky. "Remember them old days when we'd drive critters up to Abi-lene or Dodge and whoop it up and shoot it out in town after-ward? They wrote us up in the Western pulp books. Now they write up the new breed of cow spread owners in the *Wall Street Journal* or *Business Week*. Ole K. K., who died with both guns blazin', wouldn't even know the words they use these days, like 'tax shelter,' 'leverage,' 'cash basis accounting,' or 'management firm.' Did ole K. K. larn to read at all before them coyotes from the Circle Bad Guys filled him fulla lead?"

"Gol blamit, we're gittin' closer to that settin' sun, A. A.," said the trail boss. "Isn't 'gol blamit' what cowboys are sup-posed to say? Lookit the city fellers we're runnin' things fer these days. The investor who owns this lot of critters lives on a concrete range in Buffalo, New York. Probably never saw anything bigger'n a dog that had four legs on it. Certainly never saw the critters he bought yesterday. Understand he paid $100,000. Didn't have the $100,000, so he borrowed $90,000.00. They call that 'leverage.' Back in the old days a guy who ordered something for a hundred and could only come up with ten had better have his guns well greased. When you and me was young, A. A., we had to fight the sheep ranchers over our cattle grazin' land. Now them city fellers just use *our* land. Call that 'leverage,' too, I guess.

"After he shelled out $10,000.00 and signed some promissory notes with our boss—only he ain't a boss like old K. K. with them blazin' guns, he's a management company and his head man sits in a city office instead of on top of a horse—the investor got title to a lot of cows and one-third of a bull. That doesn't mean they'll carve up the bull like in a bull fight south of the border. Only that he shares services of the bull with other city-feller investors. In addition, that owner pays us (not you and me personal, A. A., but the company with its head man back in a tenth-floor office in the East) for feedin' and for managin' the herd."

"Things has changed, J. J.," said A. A., squinting up at the sky and trying for another shift in his oral cargo of terbaccy. "You and me, we don't hardly belong in this world no more."

Which is a good note on which to end the conversation between J. J. and A. A., grizzled and two-gunned trail bosses of our managed ranch. They don't belong.

But cattle do. Particularly if you are in a high enough tax bracket to enjoy the savings offered by cattle participations, them cows might belong in yore inflation-fightin' holster, podner, instead of the blazing two guns of long-dead K. K., big Western boss.

A typical investor, and the arithmetic which made his investment seem attractive, was described in a March 19, 1969 *Wall Street Journal* article on "City Cowboys":

> Modern Dairy Farms, Inc., Fort Madison, Iowa, now has 120 investors in its tax shelter program. . . . one client, a clothing

executive in the 50 percent tax bracket, bought a herd four years ago for $160,000, half of which he borrowed. He already has written the herd's value down to $60,000. . . . In addition, he receives income of $40.00 per cow per year, or $16,000 annually, on his herd of 400 head. (An equal revenue in milk sales goes to Modern Dairy Farms as a management fee; the farmer who raises the cattle keeps any remaining income.) With other deductions on the herd offsetting taxes on his milk income and then some, the investor figures to repay the $80,000 purchase loan out of milk revenues in five years, increasing his potential profit on eventual sale of the herd. This investor went to see his cows once; he recalls "slogging through the manure in the rain to take a look at the little beasts."

In that description lies one of the beauties of a cattle program, over and above the tax angle: gradual buildup of capital to make an asset stand where none stood before. The shelter angles are being whittled away by new tax provisions since that *Wall Street Journal* article was written. But they still exist in sizable part. And the buildup angle is there.

Here's what an area representative for one big management company said:

It (a cattle program) affords an outstanding opportunity for capital growth and appreciation—unique in one respect, that instead of depleting or obsoleting itself as other capital assets do, a cattle herd actually multiplies and replenishes itself. Mother Nature sees to that, with an assist from . . . professional management available, and further backed up by . . . guarantees of fertility and ten-year life span from the day of birth.

Quoting an old-hand cattle operation, *Time Magazine,* in its August 3, 1968 issue, reported:

This side of Technicolor, no one wages war on the range quite like Harold L. Oppenheimer, 47, head of the U.S.'s biggest cattle management firm. By his definition, "ranching is the nearest thing in business to a military operation. You deal with large amounts of terrain, large-scale logistics. On the battlefield as in a roundup, success depends on timing, men, and movement."

On the range, the general won his stars long ago. As founder and chairman of his Kansas City firm, Oppenheimer Industries, Inc., he maneuvers some 220,000 head of cattle on more than 100 ranches in 17 states. In addition, he is one of the nation's leading authorities on the arcane art of investing in cattle. He has written two books on ranching (*Cowboy Arithmetic, Cowboy Economics*) and co-authored a third (the recently published *Cowboy Litigation,* a 561-page tome on the tax and legal aspects of ranching).

Oppenheimer deals in cattle and feed transactions that last year amounted to $15 million and yielded nearly $1,000,000 in fees and commissions. He caters to a solvent and not exactly saddle-sore clientele (among past and present customers: Banker Robert Lehman, Comedian Jack Benny, Actress Joan Fontaine). For would-be instant cattlemen, Oppenheimer will assemble a herd, buy a spread, hire a manager and oversee the whole operation. "Real crapshooters," as Oppenheimer calls clients who are able and willing to win or lose as much as 50% on their money in a single year, can go for so-called "feeder contracts." For a down payment of $50,000 or so, Oppenheimer will handle the financing and feeding of a 500-head herd until the cattle reach proper weight and grade. The herd must then go to market, whether volatile beef prices are on the rise (which means win) or too low to cover costs (which means lose).

Safer and more strategically appealing are "breeding" contracts. "This," he says, "is where the tax play is." Taking advantage of laws that encourage the building of bigger and better herds, an Oppenheimer client can buy a 100-head breeding herd for as little as $12,000. Of that, $9,750 covers the first year's feed, financing and breeding costs, plus Oppenheimer's maximum 8½% commission—all of which is tax deductible. The remaining $1,150 represents the down payment on the herd, which, like factory machinery, is depreciable.

Unlike machines, of course, cows reproduce. After perhaps five years of tax deductions and depreciation and breeding . . . a herd can easily triple in size. When it is sold, most of the profit is taxed at the . . . capital gains rate. Investing in cows, says Oppenheimer, beats investing in oil wells.

As in the days of J. J., A. A., and K. K. with the blazin' guns, there are dangers to cattle raising. Not all is beef and profit. Old days saw droughts, rustlers, rattlesnakes, and the plain orneriness of creatures not overly blessed with thinking power. Guns eliminated some of those hazards and scientific methods make others nonoperable today. But there are still dangers to cattle investing, and the inflation hedger—city feller or knowledgeable farm boy—must be aware of these before trusting to the open (today more often closed) range as the way to make inflation say uncle.

■ Like petroleum participations, cattle programs are nonliquid. Suppose Junior breaks a leg, Susie contracts hoof and mouth disease that necessitates a hospital stay, and other sundry disasters befall you, as disasters in bunches sometimes do befall people. You cannot conveniently cash up a cattle program the way you would sell stocks or mutual funds. You can't easily borrow on it at the corner branch bank as you might on land or buildings if sudden cash needs arose. You run into something like this warning statement from the prospectus of a large cattle program operator:

> Complete herds purchased pursuant to this offering should not be expected to be readily salable. It is not expected that any public market will develop for herds as offered hereby with the attendant maintenance, replacement, and other arrangements. Complete herds will normally be transferred only in private negotiated sales to other purchasers. . . . In view of the mark-up by the Company on the sale to the herd purchaser, however, a herd purchaser should generally anticipate a loss if he resells individual animals in a market comparable to that in which the Company purchases such animals.

■ The number of animals in a herd should normally increase as nature takes its way with beasts. But the price at which animals sell is not governed by any natural law which says that it must go up. Given a glut of beef offered for sale by farmers, ranchers, and beef-raising people like you, there can be a considerable drop in beef prices. A drop like that might last for months—even longer. Nothing is sure in this world, and more cattle might sell for less dollars in the future. (Yet, beef consumption in the U.S. *is* growing; that should help future price prospects.)

■ You pick a breed and a participation program specializing in that breed—Angus, shorthorn, Santa Gertrudis, etc. Then you discover that cattle go in fashions like hemlines and stock groups, although not to so great an extent, and the breed you buy just might be replaced with a better one in greater demand. Not a likely thing over any short period of time, but something to consider.

■ Even though you turn over operation to a professional manager, it is helpful to know the trends and prospects. This means research and study on your part. The U.S. Department of Agriculture will, on request, put you on the mailing list for such publications as its *Livestock and Meat Situation*. Without some idea of what cooks with beef, your timing can be as wrong as that of a hedger who buys stocks just when a Wall Street bull market is about to break down into a bear trend.

Citrus Groves

This is another form of hedge-tax-growth play in which you don't have to know an orange from a basketball.

Citrus programs are operated much as are petroleum and cattle plays. The program is usually a limited partnership. You and other investors are the limited partners. There is also a general partner who runs things and takes his cut for doing so. Often today, these general partners are corporations rather than individuals. The days of a citrus-flavored, ruggedly individualized J. J., A. A., or K. K. are as passé in the orange patch as on the range or along Wall Street. In fact, Wall Streeters form many of the organized managements today. In 1968, a big investment house set up a subsidiary which became general partner of a citrus set-up, farming the back forty of the San Joaquin Valley in California. All officers are officers and directors of the investment firm.

Consider some of the *why* and *why not* arguments for citrus grove investing:

Why: The usual tax-shelter angle. Trees, like houses, office buildings, and other objects which do not go on forever, depreciate. Depreciation helps to afford tax shelter to citrus investments. Some farm losses reduce tax liability from nonfarm income.

Why: Professional management. It is well to be aware that no managements are exactly alike. You must try to judge management by the people in it. If they are real pros (financial professionalism might count for more than lifelong dirt-farming experience), their work won't ensure success, but it will certainly help to make success more probable.

Why: If things go right, the project should support and amortize itself. Plans call for income to cover taxes and costs and to help defray payoff on the property itself.

Why: Leverage. A typical program can be entered with 20 percent cash in your hand. If you cannot raise that amount, some participatory plans help you to borrow from the friendly management's bank even the one-fifth entry ante.

Why: Hope of an appreciation in land value. *This is a real kicker to many citrus grove investments.* Since most farm land is in California or Florida, both fast-growth states, there is enough likelihood to the kicker coming into play to make the citrus bit inviting.

Why not: The nonliquidity angle. Reread what was said about cattle programs. Change cattle to cash crop and you will have the warning of possible danger from lack of liquidity in citrus participations.

Why not: Not all groves prove profitable. This is what D. L. Brooke, Agricultural Economist of the Florida Agricultural Experimental Stations, said in a May, 1969 booklet titled, *Should I Buy a Citrus Grove?* "Over the 35-year period 18 percent of the groves studied failed to return annual operating costs, 26 percent returned from $0 to $99 per acre after deducting operating cost, 17 percent from $100 to $199, and 39 percent returned over $200 per acre after deducting operating costs."

Thus there is no guarantee of success. It might be noted, however, that Mr. Brooke wrote of operating farms, not of participating programs such as we discuss here. To help you judge productivity and price trends, the Agricultural Extension

Service of the University of Florida (Gainesville) has issued a study which might be helpful. It is called *Estimating the Value of Citrus Fruit As It Develops*. Written in 1964, its underlying principles have not changed.

Catfish Farming

Did you know that catfish out of the pond often bring more money per pound than beef, pork, or poultry?

That is why, although there are no (to my knowledge as of March 1970) participating programs for catfish farming, the idea deserves coverage as an inflation hedge. But you can't enter it for a small amount. Catfish farming takes supervision, and people who are unable to furnish this must hire it. But catfishing is a lucrative operation. Moreover, it is in a growing area which promises future success to fish farmers. You can go this deal alone or, as many do down in the catfish country, with partners so that limited burden falls upon individual partners while all participate in the profits and capital growth that each hopes will accrue.

If you don't believe that the lowly catfish is one of the growing areas of food usage, read what the magazine *Drive-In Management* said in its July 1969 issue. Titled, "Holy Mackerel! It's Catfish!" this article was not written to sell fish but to inform restaurant owners of the size of the field:

> The new catfish franchises which have suddenly started springing up around the country would have the foodservice industry believe that catfish is America's newest, hottest, up and coming food item. And they may be right. . . . Their position is based on the fact that during the last half a year some eight to ten catfish franchises have sprung up in various parts of the South. Most of them consist of a pilot operation with only one or two units under construction, but each franchisor . . . projects anywhere from 20 to 150 units in operation before this time next year. What's more, those projections include units in such cities as New York, San Francisco, Seattle and other seemingly unlikely points around the map that are *not* traditional catfish-eating areas.

TABLE 2 *Per Acre and Per Box Costs, Returns, and Other Data for Seven 5-year and One 37-year Average for Groves Averaging* 10 YEARS OF AGE A ND UNDER, 1931–68

Item	5-year averages							1931–68
	1931–36	1936–41	1941–46	1946–51	1951–56	1956–61	1961–66	
Number of grove records	55	34	20	22	18	29	49	33
Total acres of records	2387	890	472	693	1016	1151	1987	1243
Average acres per grove	43	26	24	32	55	40	41	38
Average age	8	8	7	6	4	5	7	7
Number of trees per acre	62	70	75	68	62	66	77	69
Percent trees grapefruit	24.7	30.7	16.1	12.4	13.3	5.5	0.6	13.9
Boxes harvested per acre	62	119	102	102	55	41	75	82
Costs per *acre*:								
Labor, power and equipment ...	$ 17.98	$ 23.18	$ 25.73	$ 52.56	$ 52.54	$ 60.14	$ 83.43	$ 47.23
Fertilizer materials	14.97	17.39	21.49	26.50	24.52	33.22	33.03	24.90
Spray and dust materials	2.07	3.68	4.07	4.75	4.96	8.63	15.05	7.00
State and county taxes	3.96	3.03	2.62	3.06	3.41	6.69	7.24	4.61
Miscellaneous	1.48	1.98	3.38	6.86	7.83	8.08	5.89	5.00
Total operating costs	40.46	49.26	57.29	93.73	93.26	116.76	144.64	88.74
Interest on grove valuation @ 6%	25.32	26.94	22.50	25.05	31.33	41.61	69.19	37.42
Total cost without owner supervision	65.78	76.20	79.79	118.78	124.59	158.37	213.83	126.16

5-year averages

	1931-36	1936-41	1941-46	1946-51	1951-56	1956-61	1961-66	1931-68
Returns per *acre*:								
Returns from fruit	50.11	84.36	170.70	134.71	67.54	88.40	143.20	109.21
Net returns	−15.67	8.16	90.91	15.93	−57.05	−69.97	−70.63	−16.95
Returns above operating costs ..	9.65	35.10	113.41	40.98	−25.72	−28.36	− 1.44	20.47
Costs per *box*:								
Labor, power and equipment ...	.29	.19	.25	.51	.96	1.47	1.11	.58
Fertilizer materials	.24	.15	.21	.26	.45	.81	.44	.30
Spray and dust materials	.04	.03	.04	.05	.09	.21	.20	.08
State and county taxes	.06	.02	.03	.03	.06	.16	.10	.06
Miscellaneous	.02	.02	.03	.07	.14	.20	.08	.06
Total operating costs	.65	.41	.56	.92	1.70	2.85	1.93	1.08
Interest on grove valuation @ 6%	.41	.23	.22	.25	.57	1.01	.92	.46
Total cost without owner supervision	1.06	.64	.78	1.17	2.27	3.86	2.85	1.54
Returns per *box*:								
Returns from fruit	.81	.71	1.67	1.32	1.23	2.16	1.91	1.33
Net returns	−.25	.07	.89	.15	−1.04	−1.70	− .94	−.21
Returns above operating costs ...	.16	.30	1.11	.40	− .47	− .69	− .02	.25

SOURCE: *Thirty-seven Years of Citrus Costs and Returns in Florida, 1931–1968,* by D. L. Brooke, Agricultural Economist, Florida Agricultural Experiment Station. Issued September, 1969.

Those are mighty heady projections on behalf of a bewhisk-ered, bull-faced, mud-loving scavenger. Yet four factors remove those projections from the realm of mere speculation and into the cold light of reality: 1) there has been an inordinate amount of action among catfish franchises. 2) The source of supply has undergone a radical change. Catfish farming is supplanting the traditional methods of dredging wild water lakes and rivers. 3) Breeding innovations, along with controlled feeding, are pro-ducing a better tasting product. 4) New merchandising tech-niques are introducing the product into ever-widening geo-graphical areas. . . . there has also been a marked increase in catfish consumption. The product has been added to the menus of several major franchises including the Mahalia Jackson Chicken System, James Brown's Golden Platter and a number of other organizations which operate drive-ins in catfish-eating parts of the nation or franchises in ghetto areas. One pilot unit . . . claims to have grossed $14,000 in its third month of opera-tions. In 1968, according to the U.S. Dept. of the Interior's Bureau of Commercial Fisheries, some 80 million pounds of cat-fish was sold in the United States. By 1975 the Bureau estimates that this figure will double; 160 million pounds will be sold. The bulk of the fish goes on the retail market for cooking at home. Almost all the rest is sold to commercial restaurants.

Why this sudden interest in a product that most people outside of the South think of as a poor people's food? Because, with the advent of catfish farming, the source of supply can finally be controlled and produced in quantities adequate to meet market demands. The product itself has also undergone a change in taste, texture and eye-appeal.

The catfish can grow anywhere. As long ago as September 22, 1967 the *Kansas Academy of Science* reported on "Production and Growth of Channel Catfish Fry," a paper by O. W. Tie-meier, C. W. Deyoe, and C. Suppes. *Drive-in Management* pointed out that cats can be grown anywhere in the United States, even on top of mountains.

Since this field is not known to everyone who savors beef or eats grapefruit with his breakfast, a short bibliography of cat-fish farming publications can help you. Start with the Catfish

Farmers of America publication, *The Catfish Farmer*. It comes out quarterly and a subscription is available from the Association's office in the Tower Bldg., Little Rock, Ark.

Write also for *Catfish Farming Profit Opportunities* from the Mississippi Research and Development Center, 787 Lakeland Dr., Jackson, Miss. Ask Thibault Milling Co. (P. O. Box 549, Little Rock) for *Guide to Profitable Catfish Farming*. The State Fish Hatchery at Centerton, Ark., has *Propagation of Channel Catfish,* and the U.S. Dept. of Agriculture offers *Pond Construction and Economic Considerations in Catfish Farming,* a paper by Roy A. Grizzell, Jr., Soil Conservation Service biologist.

Catfish farmers are eager people. They hold a whole new industry by its finny tail. Their enthusiasm should not let you fail to note that catfish farming, like other inflation hedges, has drawbacks and dangers as well as opportunities.

■ Says the U.S. Department of the Interior's Fish and Wildlife Service in a booklet on farm reservoir fishes: "This fish (channel cat) is in great demand as a food fish. Unfortunately, the artificial propagation of the species requires special techniques and farmers usually must purchase fingerlings from commercial breeders. In general, two or three growing seasons are required to produce a marketable crop."

■ Dat ol' debbil, nonliquidity, is present in this field. If you own a catfish farm, you can't call a broker and say, "Sell!" when you want out or require funds. Worse, if you are in this with partners, as are so many investors and inflation hedgers who do the catfish bit, then you will have even more difficulty in selling a slice of a cat farm than you would encounter as sole owner of the ponds, fingerlings, and land.

■ The investment is not small. However, it can be financed as are other kinds of real estate.

■ No professional management is currently available. You will have to learn how and do it yourself (or with partners and assistants). The other side of this coin shows that you, not a J. J., A. A., or K. K., reap the management share of profits.

TABLE 3   *Channel Catfish Fingerling Production—Eight-acre Opera-tion—Pond Spawn Method*

Initial Costs

Construction of ponds, 22,500 yds. @ 20¢	$ 4,500.00
Drain pipes	312.00
Well costs $1,400.00 ⎫	
Pump 1,500.00 ⎬ To serve 40 acres	3,700.00
Motor 800.00 ⎭	
70 pairs of brood fish (420 pounds @ $1.00)	420.00

Annual Costs

Pond construction and pipe amortized @ 6% for 20 yrs. ($4,812.00 × .08718)	$ 419.51
Well amortized @ 6% for 20 yrs. (1,400.00 × .08718 ÷ 5)*..	24.41
Pump amortized @ 6% for 15 yrs. ($1,500.00 × .10296 ÷ 5)* .	30.88
Motor amortized @ 6% for 4 yrs. ($800.00 × .28859 ÷ 5)*...	46.17
*Prorated to 40-acre operation.	
Annual maintenance on well, pump, and motor (prorated) .	85.00
Pond maintenance	35.25
Pumping costs, 6 acre-feet × 8 acres = 48 acre-feet × $11.20	537.60
Brood fish amortized @ 6% for 4 yrs. ($420.00 × .28859)	121.20
Feed—12 tons of pellets @ $92.00 ton	1,104.00
1,000 pounds minnow meal @ $98.00 ton	49.00
Rent	100.00
Equipment purchases (prorated)	148.00
Transportation—feeding and hauling	150.00
Labor costs—feeding and daily checking	480.00
harvesting	500.00
Total Costs of Production	$ 3,831.02

Gross Returns

200,000 fingerlings @ 0.07 ea...........................	$14,000.00
Less costs of production	3,831.02

Net Returns—to land and management (8 acres)	$10,168.98
Average net return per acre	1,271.12
Costs of producing fingerlings (each)	0.018

Feed Conversion: 5.8:1

SOURCE: "Pond Construction and Economic Considerations in Catfish Farm-ing," a paper presented at the 21st Southeastern Ass'n of Game and Fish Commissioners, New Orleans, La., Sept. 25–27, 1967, by Roy A. Grizzell, Jr., Biologist, Soil Conservation Service, USDA.

SEVEN QUESTIONS:

Q. *Doesn't the new (1969) Federal income tax law curtail some shelter advantages of so-called "weekend farming"?*

A. Yes. The new law inhibits but doesn't stop your ability to offset some regular income with farming losses. The big difference comes when the yearly loss gets above $25,000 and if nonfarm income tops $50,000.

Q. *How do I buy a cattle, catfish, or citrus program?*

A. Many regular brokerage houses offer cattle and citrus farming participations. You can also watch the ads in financial publications and other periodicals and get in direct touch with managements. If you buy in large dollar amounts, management may invite you out to have a look around the farmsteads where cattle graze and citrus trees bud.

Catfish farms are a different thing. At the time of this writing (March 1970) no programs are available as in oil, cows, or citrus. You have to start your own. Often friends and associates who like the notion of profit as well as sauce piquante atop fish dishes organize their own partnerships.

Q. *Why speak of a catfish "farm"? It isn't like growing corn or wheat.*

A. It is exactly like growing corn or wheat. In one case the farmer plows the ground, puts in seed, adds fertilizer, tends, and then harvests a crop when it has grown to marketable size.

The owner of a catfish farm likewise prepares the ground. He does this by making a pond instead of plowing a row. He then puts in small fish instead of seed, adds fish feed instead of chemical or organic fertilizer, weeds out trash fish instead of trash vegetation, and when the crop has grown to what he considers marketable size, he harvests them and sells the crop.

Q. *Isn't the catfish a scavenger? Who wants to eat him?*

A. You have in mind the old species that infested polluted waters. These are a different breed of cat (*ictalurus punctatus*). Channel catfish grown in clean ponds are related to the old mud cat in the same way modern man is related to Cro-Magnon —by ancestry.

Q. *What is done about breeding cows I receive under a cattle program?*

A. Says the prospectus of a leading management company:

> The Company undertakes to breed all female animals sold to a Herd owner as early as possible consistent with sound breeding practice and the registration requirements of the American Angus Association. Although female animals may be bred earlier, the Company recommends that they be at least 15 months of age prior to first insemination, and that male animals' semen not be collected until they are between 1½ to 2 years of age. In accordance with industry practice, female animals initially sold by the Company are entitled to one initial successful breeding with bulls of the Company specified by it. The bull used for this purpose will be one of approximately 20 leading bulls owned by the Company or in which it has an interest. After the first breeding, however, a Herd owner, if he is to obtain progeny registerable under the rules of the American Angus Association, must use the semen of a bull in which he owns an interest with no more than two other owners owning the balance of the interests in the bull.

Q. *What is a feedlot? Will I need one?*

A. A feedlot is a place where cattle are fattened. You won't need one in most cases if you participate in a limited-partnership cattle program.

Q. *Please define "citrus."*

A. Citrus fruits are lemons, oranges, grapefruit, tangerines— in general, breakfast-table fruit. Some citrus groves in which investors participate raise almonds and other nuts along with citrus fruits.

9

Oats and Orange Juice Can Be Better than Money

1969 WAS NOT A HAPPY YEAR for most investors who traded in the stock market. Many lost from 25 percent to 50 percent of their capital by not heeding the fact that no one should hold stocks through a bear market. Nor was it a joyous twelve months for brokers who handled their buy and sell orders. Many of the latter dropped from profit positions to no-profit positions despite the high average level of commission volume. Some of the brokers, however, fared better than their investor clients. Those who also had memberships on the commodity exchanges enjoyed commissions from trading volume that soared around 20 percent.

Commodities are becoming a big, "in" area for trading. They are an effective inflation hedge as well. But you have to know the rules for success; it is a tricky trade.

This chapter will examine opportunities in two kinds of commodities. One is the intangible kind of "futures" contract exemplified by wheat, soybeans, eggs, or cocoa. The other is more tangible. Examples are scotch whisky, art objects, new wines, stamps, diamonds, and coins. The last five require expert judgment for sound selection. For the scotch, the rationale is that usquebagh isn't soon going out of American drinking fashion.

What Are "Intangible" Commodities?

We are discussing orange juice and oats, pork bellies and live cattle, plywood, wool, potatoes, rye, soybeans, palladium, platinum, silver, copper, cocoa, sugar to sweeten it, cotton, eggs, flaxseed, barley, broilers, meal, and corn. There isn't anything intangible about an orange or an ear of corn. Few inflation hedgers who take the commodity approach, however, graze cattle on their lawns or stuff carloads of pork bellies into their home freezers. Nor do they stockpile orange juice or precious platinum. They buy "futures."

A futures contract is a deal by which, if you are "long" (in other words, if you own the contract), you pay a set price for an extremely large amount of the commodity deliverable in the future. You can be "short" the commodity; in that, you are in the position of offering that same large lot to the other fellow who bought your short.

Sounds complicated, but it is not.

example Assume you buy a contract of December wheat at 145, a price at which it was available on the day this was written and an average sort of price for wheat. You have become—not yet the owner—but the fellow who, if he still is long the contract when the December delivery date rolls around, will be tendered 5,000 bushels of wheat. Nobody is going to back up a railroad car (the approximate size of 5,000 bushels) to your door and begin spreading wheat around your lawn as if it were humus. Instead, you will be given a warehouse receipt for your wheat. And you will be asked for more money. A lot of it.

Typically, such a wheat contract might trade on margin of $700. Margin is a good-faith payment and a cushion which allows your broker room in which to cash you up in case things go sufficiently against you when you're wrong about price trend that the loss begins to eat into *his* capital. If you hold your wheat contract until delivery time, you will be asked for the rest of the money to become proud owner of a warehouse filled with grain. You can then try eating the stuff, sell it as "spot" wheat, or take your city friends around to see what the grain out of which their bread is made looks like when in the raw, untreated state.

But nobody lets things go so far. You aren't in the market to take delivery on the wheat unless you are a wheat processor instead of an inflation hedger. You want to deal in the contract.

That makes you a speculator, and you had better understand the fact very early. Trading in commodity futures may be done through the same broker from whom you purchase and through whom you sell stocks, bonds, or mutual funds. You can hold the bonds until they mature. You can hold the stocks and mutuals until hell freezes over, until you tire of looking at the color ink with which the certificates are printed, or until (if you're smart and follow suggestions in earlier chapters) there appear signs telling you that the stock or fund has had it and should be replaced with a better and possibly prettier investment.

Not so with commodity contracts.

The reason is that futures contracts expire.

The December contract means nothing after its December expiration. The March contract takes off its Cinderella ball clothes and becomes a stodgy warehouse receipt after midnight of the March day of expiration. Then you are a wheat man, not an investor, trader, inflation fighter, or speculator. The commodity futures game is for a relatively short term, which might be six days, six weeks, or (rarely) six months. Not six years or eternity.

Commodity futures can help as a hedge against dwindling of the dollar, always provided that you trade intelligently (this chapter will tell you how) and provided that you keep in mind and repeat each morning as you prepare to greet the new day: "I am a commodity speculator. I am a trader. I am *not* an investor for the long term when I trade commodity futures contracts."

You deal not in cocoa (excepting those in the chocolate business) but in cocoa contracts. You are not interested in orange juice unless you have a voracious breakfast thirst, but in contracts for frozen orange juice. When the future for these commodities becomes the present, you run, man, run. Nothing is long in term of years about futures trading, although much about it can be useful, even highly profitable, to an inflation hedger interested in keeping ahead over the years.

When you go long, you do so in expectation that the price of the contract will rise before it expires. Then you sell the contract itself, and if it has increased in price, you pocket a profit. When you go short, it is done in expectation that the price will drop before contract expiration. If the price goes down, you "cover" by purchasing the commodity you earlier sold, at a lower price than you sold it, thus harvesting a profit. Over the life of any contract astute commodity traders are likely to be both long and short on different occasions. When they are wise in their judgment of price trends, they can garner a profit in both directions even though the commodity contract at the end of the period in which they both shorted and bought long may be exactly, to the tenth of a penny, what it was at the start of the upside-downside play.

The margin in a commodity futures contract is very small. Seven hundred dollars to swing 5,000 bushels of wheat constitutes only a tiny portion of its value. You don't borrow the rest of the money and pay interest, as you would do in purchasing stocks on margin, because nothing has been lent to you. Nobody—as noted—owns the wheat at that point. Leverage of this kind is wonderful when you win. It allows parlaying of a small stake into a fortune. But leverage is blind. It doesn't know whether you win or lose. If you win, it magnifies the gain. If you lose, leverage as faithfully—perhaps joyously—magnifies your loss. There are histories of people who ran small sums into big estates through this kind of leveraging. Unhappily, there are as many, perhaps more, cases of fortunes being reduced to small sums by the effect of leverage when the trader was wrong. We will look next at ways of putting the probabilities on your side. These methods won't always work, but they will help and, if followed carefully, should put you in the minority of people who win in the commodity markets.

Principal exchanges on which commodity futures contracts trade are: Board of Trade in Chicago; Chicago Mercantile Exchange; Commodity Exchange; New York Cocoa Exchange; New York Coffee and Sugar Exchange; New York Cotten Exchange; New York Mercantile Exchange; New York Produce Exchange. There are smaller exchanges where commodity futures contracts are traded in Kansas City, Minneapolis, and Winnipeg.

A Trading Plan for Futures Contracts

You have two ways to analyze the prospects for a futures contract moving up or down, and you should employ both. One is called "fundamental." The other is termed "technical."

Enthusiasts for the technical approach scorn fundamentals and laugh at their fundamentalist brethren. Dedicated fundamentalists think all followers of charting and technical approaches are woozy in the head and not to be trusted on the street without a white-coated attendant following close behind.

As so often happens with extremist thinking on any side of a question, when you carry an argument that far, you are likely to have overlooked something. The commodity trading enthusiasts overlook the fact that both disciplines can be practiced. The fellow who has two views of a planned investment should be better off than the one who looks at it from only one side.

In an earlier book, *Nine Roads to Wealth* (McGraw-Hill), I touched upon ways to look at commodities from a fundamental viewpoint. Six questions were suggested. Answers to these can put you on the right inflation-hedging path:

1. *What is the background business climate?* If recession looms, probabilities are that few things will go up. If a new boom appears to be beginning, it can carry commodity prices along in its wake particularly if . . . boom brings inflation. But don't look only at the Stateside business climate. Many commodities move in international channels. . . . Worldwide conditions should be weighed and judged.

2. *What is probable production this year?* How much crop carry-over from last year? Until a crop is in, or the amount of overseas commodity which will be marketed is known, this remains conjecture. After it is known, of course, it ceases to be a market factor affecting prices because the price structure will have already taken it into account. While you cannot know the future until it happens, you can use some knowledgeable appraisals of prospects.

(Many necessary fundamental facts are available in publications of the United States Department of Agriculture. Specifically, the following can be helpful: *Agricultural Outlook Digest, Demand and Price Situation, Cotton Situation, Dairy Situation, Fats and Oil Situation, Feed Situation, Fruit Situation, Livestock and Meat Situation, Poultry and Egg Situation, Vegetable Situation, Wheat Situation, Wool Situation, National Food Situation, World Agricultural Situation.* To go deeper into commodity economics, get the quarterly *Agricultural Economics Research.* Brokerage houses also issue private appraisals, and many of these are excellent. Finally, there are commodity newsletters and services.)

3. *What are demand prospects?*

Sometimes appraisals are nothing but educated guesses. However, any serious appraisal is better than none, and if you do not feel able to decide how many million bushels of wheat will be shipped overseas and how many will end in the form of instant breakfast foods to be used in this country, you might get the professional appraisals of three or four sources—taking in a commodity advisor or commodity market letter plus the research appraisals from brokerage sources—and average them off. Some traders say this is a sound way to do a job for which there is no scientific basis.

4. *Can competitive products eat into the probable market?*

Soybean and other vegetable oils can be used almost alternatively. A scarcity situation in one will not automatically bring about higher prices as long as glut exists in the alternatives.

5. *What is the current news saying?* When Chile or Zambia decides to nationalize copper, the result might be a future shortage. But not automatically. For if the nation which now controls the product should decide to meet an immediate capital need by flooding world markets from its stockpiles, the quicker result could be lower prices.

Governments' agricultural policies affect pricing and must be watched. Wars have widespread effects. Sometimes the chain reactions from shortages due to combat or destruction can widen out to touch unexpected commodities.

Currency devaluations act upon the ability of a country to buy American and Canadian commodities. They change the prices of products a nation exports. Usually the aim of devaluation is to make local products more competitive in global markets.

6. *What are seasonal tendencies?* Many commodities tend toward price weaknesses at certain seasons of the year, and their prices reach high levels at others. This tendency is seldom strong enough to make it the basis for a trading system in itself. But it exists and should be taken into account. No one wants to be long in a commodity in May when the historic trend of May-to-July prices is downward.

In Chapter Three, we looked at support and resistance levels and at trend lines. These are the main tools of the technically minded commodity trader. Chartists follow a host of patterns which emerge upon their ruled paper. There are "head and shoulders" tops and bottoms; "rounding turns"; "triangles"; "rectangles"; "double tops and double bottoms." If you remember the lessons of support and resistance study and what a trend line is and how to judge movements out of trend line, however, you will find that these underlie every kind of charting pattern and formation. Technical stock study applies to commodity timing as it does to stocks.

To wrap fundamental and technical study methods together into a unified strategy, buy (go long) only when the fundamentals appear to favor a shortage and price appreciation and when there has also been a significant breakout from a resistance level or the penetration of a longer-term trend line. Every little toddle above or below a line is not significant. A meaningful move is one which breaks through a level either several times "tested" by having stopped other attempts to rise, or one which earlier stopped a rise of really major (as opposed to day-to-day) importance. A significant trend line break would be one going through a longer-term trend line, not one drawn to delineate a minor movement.

Go short only after observing these directions in reverse.

But don't act unless both areas of study bring out the same answer. If the fundamentals look strong but there is no corresponding technical strength, you may get a big profit by playing it fast without waiting for your timing tools to confirm. Before you decide on such a policy, reread what was said about commodity leverage. Leverage makes a mistake expensive. You want to conserve your capital, not fritter it away trading on moves that are not strong and may not be long.

Remember that your losses must be cut—fast, while small. Typically, a commodity trader can find himself wrong and therefore losing money on half of his commitments. But if he lets the profits run instead of foolishly grabbing at any small gain, and if he then cuts losses severely and swiftly, he can make great increments accrue to his starting capital.

In stocks there is a way to institutionalize your activities through mutual funds. The mutual fund idea is now moving into commodities. As a mutualization technique, however, this is new. It behooves an inflation fighter to look carefully into the record of any commodity trading fund before he hands over capital to an unknown manager to trade for him.

Offbeat, Tangible Commodities

"Scotch whisky," a friend told me, "is wonderful stuff. It makes a nice sociable drink. People worried about inflation can drown their troubles in it when they see Johnny's tuition for high school up again, or that the price of eggs in the supermarket has trebled. Really smart people who are worried about inflation don't do this, however. They invest in scotch warehouse receipts. Appreciation in these more than beats the decline in dollar purchasing power." If you listen to enthusiasts like my friend, scotch seems a foolproof hedge. When it works, it can be as profitable as these enthusiasts claim. But it has some dangers, too.

The game of inflation hopscotch is played with warehouse receipts. All scotch, by law, must be aged a minimum of three years. Most is aged longer. The distiller ties up enormous amounts of capital in his warehouses, and anything that can free some of this for regular business use, and at the same time provide profit, is welcome. Enter the warehouse receipt purchaser.

There are two kinds of scotch. One is grain whisky. The grains are something like vodka; they have no taste and are used to blend with the second kind of whisky, malt, to produce many scotches. Some scotch whiskies are blends of malts only. You will have to do some homework on the probable demand-supply situation in both kinds before deciding upon which to buy.

Let's say you've purchased malt. You expect to hold it for four years. At the end of that time you expect that by aging it will have increased in value. Some brokers in scotch receipts say it should bring an average of 25 percent a year this way. Such an accrual of value is more than enough to fight inflation. Assume the expectation is correct (shortly, we will look at the chances of your being wrong and losing instead of gaining on this "sure" scotch investment).

Four years later you have a choice. Under one plan you can buy an equal amount of new zero-age malt whisky warehouse receipts and pocket the difference in cash. If you do this, you will pay capital gains tax instead of being taxed at ordinary income rates (unless tax laws change). This adds to current spending power and you will still have the stake in aging scotch to turn over again.

Or you can do it another way. You swap the receipt for now-aged whisky for the dollar value in new whisky receipts. You will then have a greater number of receipts, and if all goes well with your expectation, you will be in a position in a few years to do the gambit again. Possibly, your capital will increase at (1) the rate of increase in value as the whisky ages and (2) the plowed-back rate, which adds additional receipts to your portfolio of scotch.

One receipt dealer has recommended that clients buy the same number of receipts for malt each year during four straight years. At the end of that time, he points out, clients can either achieve a steady year-to-year income boost by following course (1), or geometrically increase their capital by following course (2). It sounds very good. Indeed, it has been a profitable ploy for many people. But you should not attempt either course (1) or course (2) without realizing that there is nothing inevitably profitable about scotch whisky inflation hedging. What follows is pointed out, not to discourage the use of scotch as an inflation hedge, but to warn that it, like other hedging methods, can bring about loss:

During some of the years of the 1960's, when the glamour of being a whisky owner by the warehouseful had hit investors along with the idea that the use of scotch would never die, receipt prices suddenly took a plunge.

The brisk market had encouraged some distillers to increase production in order to obtain whisky on which warehouse receipts could be sold to eager investors. Soon receipts glutted the market. Adding to the drop in price, some had been held with heavy loans on them, and when they declined, hard-headed bankers sold the receipts to save their loans. That further depressed the market.

The market appears well on its way back, and scotch receipts, handled with due caution and an awareness that nothing in this life is surefire, can serve as an effective inflation container. So can other forms of tangible commodities.

Fortunes have been made in art, rare objects, stamps, wine, and diamonds. By their use, some people have not only nullified the effects of dollar inflation but turned that inflation's action upon art into a builder of vast fortunes.

These investors shared one characteristic. *Each understood the field thoroughly.* Because that sentence is the key to avoiding heavy loss, as well as—if you are truly an expert—making gains, I want to repeat it.

Vast fortunes can be made by using paintings, diamonds, and other jewelry, objets d'art, wines, and rare stamps as inflation hedges. But the only people likely to succeed are those who know the fields thoroughly.

If you are one who does know those areas, you need no information here on how to use them as inflation hedges. If you do not know them, you need this advice: Either become an expert—a process taking years—or avoid such tangibles. Inexpert judgment leads to losses. Nonliquidity affects your ability to turn a Renoir, however treasured, into cash. I knew a man twenty years ago who purchased a genuine, certificated Rubens for $10,000. Much of this kind of art has appreciated to seven-figure values. My friend's Rubens, alas, sits in a safe place eating up rentals and he has been unable to realize what he feels such a rare treasure to be worth.

TEN QUESTIONS:

Q. *What do commodity people mean by "overtrading" a market?*

A. The same thing a physical education major means by over-training an athlete: doing it too much. Trying to catch every minor swing. Trading all of the time instead of trading only when the probabilities of a rise or decline are strongly on your side. If an athlete overtrains, he gets stale. If you overtrade, you are likely to defeat your purpose by piling up higher commissions, taking smaller profits when you are right, and being wrong a greater percentage of the time than is necessary.

Q. *Are commodity futures markets government-regulated for public protection?*

A. The regulatory body is the Commodity Exchange Authority, not the Securities and Exchange Commission, as with stocks, bonds, and mutual funds. The CEA is an arm of the U.S. Department of Agriculture. Commodity exchanges themselves have stringent rules to protect the public.

Q. *Are there regulations on trading of scotch whisky, stamps, objets d'art, etc.?*

A. Other than the regular laws which define and punish fraud, there are no regulations covering these trades. The Securities and Exchange Commission has expressed interest in defining whether scotch warehouse receipts under some circumstances might become "securities" within the meaning of its law.

Q. *Are managed commodity accounts the answer to successful commodity trading by a rank novice?*

A. They can be, depending upon how successful, knowledgeable, and generally hip are the people who do the managing. Some firms in this field can boast successful records. If you put your capital into an account giving anyone else discretion over what you do, you had better form some judgment of the manager. Even with good will, good faith, and integrity, all professional traders don't succeed with other people's capital.

Q. *For short sales to be successful, prices of commodities would have to drop. Doesn't a drop in commodity prices tend to end inflation and the problem with which we are concerned?*

A. Not necessarily.

We don't buy potatoes, wash them, peel them, and cook them to the extent our parents did. Increasingly, we get food in a frozen or pre-prepared state. All the convenience cooked into convenience packages has to be paid for. The result is that the cost of the food itself constitutes a lesser proportion of the supermarket checkout ticket, and the cost of freezing it, cooking it, packaging it, drying it, and instantizing it counts for more and more. A decrease in commodity prices might lessen inflation, but only to a small extent. Keep in mind, too, that the drop in prices for which a trader goes short is likely to be a movement lasting one to six months. That has little long-term inflationary effect.

This was noted in the December 1969 *Monthly Review* of the Federal Reserve Bank of Atlanta in a report titled, "Farm Prices Have Drifted Downward; Will Consumers Benefit?":

> That consumer food prices tend to stick at high levels is clearly demonstrated. Increases in wholesale farm prices are nearly always accompanied by rising consumer food prices. *The latter are slow to decline, however, when wholesale prices drop. In fact, lower wholesale prices are usually reflected in the consumer price index by a slower rate of increase or sidewise movement.* [italics supplied]

Q. *What prevents me from taking receipt when a commodity becomes spot and THEN waiting for the price rise I expect to come? Wouln't I then be able to hold commodities over many years?*

A. Depending upon the commodity, you would indeed be able to hold it over many years. Whether it would then prove an inflation hedge, however, is doubtful.

Commodity futures trading is attractive because of its leverage. The leverage is there only when you consider profits in relation to the margin put up. When gain has to be computed as a percentage of the total price of a commodity, then such trading offers less than worthwhile opportunities. And you would have the factors of storage fees and insurance working to diminish that profit.

Q. *How good is the commodity information a brokerage house puts out?*

A. As with the comment on managed accounts, this depends upon the reliability and good judgment of the source. A great deal of brokerage house data is excellent. It has one drawback. It is widely disseminated; therefore many people act upon it. Information everyone—or a sizable proportion of traders—acts upon tends to be self-defeating.

Q. *Projections indicate commodity trading may become more popular in future. Won't that remove some of the swinging attraction of these volatile markets?*

A. Perhaps. But it will not remove the big element of leverage, which supplies most of that swinging attraction. Movements in relation to margin put up make commodity markets swing, seldom the size of the moves in relation to absolute price level.

Q. *Are there regular price quotes on scotch whisky warehouse receipts?*

A. They do not trade on an exchange such as the Chicago Board of Trade or New York Mercantile. There is a vague over-the-counter market. It is at best thin and you can't count on great liquidity in these instruments.

Q. *Some say that in the future scotch will be imported in bulk rather than by the bottle. Will this affect the value of warehouse receipts?*

A. Probably not.

The reason for bulk importation is that U.S. law assesses tariffs on whisky by bulk, not alcoholic content. It therefore becomes economic to bring in the booze at 120 proof, then cut it to the 80 to 86 proof at which scotch usually sells, and bottle it in the U.S. The trend is increasing. But not all scotch brands are brought in this way. The process should not have great effect upon future pricing of warehouse receipts. Growth or decline in scotch consumption is a more important figure to watch.

10

It Helps to Mind Your Business

FOR DECADES, the ocean liner *Queen Mary* and a sister, *Queen Elizabeth,* reigned over the Atlantic waves. During World War II, they carried immense numbers of troops abroad for victory over the Axis. But in 1968, the mighty *Queen Mary's* innards were up for grabs. A smart Los Angeles designer, Gene Darcy, made the winning grab—and was on his way to a fortune in an unusual business.

Today, the *Queen Mary* serves as a floating motel in Long Beach (California) harbor. Plumbing and fixtures, luxurious in 1936, have been replaced with more modern American fittings. The insides so unceremoniously yanked out of the queenly liner soon adorned Darcy-owned stores in San Francisco, Chicago, and New Orleans, where in early 1970 they were bringing

$12.50 for a two-foot length of mooring line, $32.50 for a deck chair, or $40.00 for a chamber pot, all bought by the alert Darcy at scrap prices. The three stores deal exclusively in appurtenances from the *Queens*.

Darcy's success illustrates what your own business can do to hedge against inflation. Scrap from the *Queen Mary* and *Queen Elizabeth* is not available to everyone. We don't all have Gene Darcy's quick grasp of potential in an unusual business. But a business of one's own is a possibility for everyone.

The beauty of a business is that, if successful, it expands to inflation rates. However, not everyone is qualified by either temperament or knowledge to run his own business. If you are one of those who are happiest on a payroll, the subject of this chapter would not be the best of the inflation-fighting hedges. Yet, the range of possible businesses is so wide that most people can find something, and many sideline businesses have expanded to full-time, big-profit enterprises.

To determine whether the owner-manager bit is for you, a thorough checklist was compiled by staff members of the U.S. Small Business Administration. It asks such general questions as:

What are your chances of success?
Are you the type?
Where should you locate?
Should you buy a going business?
How much capital will you need?
Should you share ownership with others?
How will you manage personnel?
What records should you keep?
Are you qualified to supervise buying and selling?
How will you price your products and services?
What laws will affect you?
What other problems will you face?
Will you keep up to date?

"After I waded through that kind of self-interrogation I was so scared I nearly went back to the safety of a salary and almost threw up the idea of self-employment," one now-successful thirty-year-old entrepreneur told me. "It was frightening. But it was helpful too, and before I had been in business two years I knew how vital was this initial thinking-out process."

A startling percentage of new businesses go broke in their first years. Poor advance thinking undoubtedly accounts for many failures. A U.S. Department of Commerce study blamed inadequate record-keeping for many failures. "Bookkeeping isn't fun unless you are a trained accountant," said my entrepreneurial friend, "but, wow!—how necessary. Without it you don't know where you are nor where you're headed. Anyone who finds figures too dull isn't going to make it in a business of his own."

Franchising, to which we will shortly come, is one field of new-business start-up which saves you much of the bookkeeping plans, although it won't exempt you from bookkeeping chores. Statistics show that a franchised new business has considerably better chance of early success than one you start on your own. According to Al Lapin, head of International Industries, "a successful franchisor does not sell hamburgers or chicken, he sells a business system. The franchise method of distribution can be applied to almost any . . . business consistent with its size—not too big for an unsophisticated businessman, but not so small he's just buying a job." That is why fewer franchisees fail. They buy successful systems with each step planned in advance and proved in operation.

You may like the franchise approach, or you may prefer to go with your own idea, as did ingenious Gene Darcy and as do thousands of less unusual plumbers, retailers, and service technicians who rely upon the sales growth at steady profit margins afforded by a going business to counter the effect of inflation's dollar dwindle.

Self-employment in your own business can be lonely. There is seldom anyone with whom to share decision responsibility. But it can be rewarding in more ways than one.

What Are Your Chances of Making It?

If you keep in mind that you are after profits and not merely sales; that you seek only contracts and orders that will pay off on the last line of the profit-loss statement; that you are in business to generate lettuce of the kind that goes into a bank account and not merely serve people with produce—then you have the key to answering the question about business chances with two words: "Pretty good."

In a Small Business Administration *Small Marketers Aid* of August 1962, reprinted January 1967, and as valid in 1972 as 1962, Frederick G. Disney, a management consultant of Fort Worth, Texas, wrote:

> Net profit is probably the most important indicator of the success of a business operation. Hence you should be concerned about the reliability of that figure. You can be surer of its accuracy by understanding the principal ways in which profits can be erroneously stated. Basically, there are four areas in which you can kid yourself about your profits.
>
> 1. *The Existence of a Profit.* Key question: Are such items as depreciation and inventory handled realistically in the accounting system?
>
> 2. *The Sufficiency of the Profit.* Key question: Although you may be making a profit, can it be considered sufficient for your size and type of operation?
>
> 3. *The Profit Mix.* Key question: Although you may be showing a good profit from your total operation, are there lines or departments in the company which are actually losing money?
>
> 4. *The Profit Trend.* Key question: Does the trend of profit show healthy progress, or is the tendency towards less and less profit?

Find the Right Business

If you go into a field you know, the chances for success are immeasurably greater than if you happily skip into an area where you are unaware of the booby traps and don't know the rules of traffic. Yet, people have been successful in fields entirely new to them. In almost every case, however, these successful innovators into fresh areas are people who took time to study everything about that new field before being beguiled by green, green grass on someone else's side of a fence.

Discover where the public's money is currently being spent. Some consumer buying studies are national and wouldn't apply to the plans of people in Tadpole, Texas, who have different customs, incomes, and needs from those in Whistlestop, Wyoming or Aridity, Arizona. Localized surveys are often made by the colleges of business administration of state universities. Write to the dean at your state university for help.

On the national scene, a good guide is the *Consumer Buying Prospects* put out quarterly by Commercial Credit Co., 300 St. Paul Place, Baltimore, Md. Write the Superintendent of Documents, Government Printing Office, Washington, D.C., for the Bureau of the Census' quarterly *Consumer Buying Indicators.*

Some people who dine on pheasant and live in hilltop mansions above a rolling countryside made their piles without studying such consumer planning guides as these. They went the government contracts route. There can be danger in such an approach. Government contracts, available to small businesses as well as large, are frequently switched, choked off, or redirected at only momentary notice. The plant set up to meet one federal agency's need for putty knives can become a white elephant in jig time when the putty knife plan is changed and wimwams are in demand instead. If you decide to go after government contracts despite these dangers, the U.S. Department of Commerce can assist with lists of government requirements.

Merchandise you sell can be anything from lots to locomotives. (I recall one gentleman who made an excellent annual income selling used choo-choos and the supplies needed to keep them chugging, by catering to sawmills and others with short-trackage hauling requirements.) If you opt to sell a service, it might be your own specialty in whatever form it comes. The personnel manager seeking a new field can become training adviser to medium-sized companies. The purchasing agent can run a service to put together small orders from little companies so that his clients achieve economies of scale while he achieves inflation-fighting business fees. The list of service possibilities is endless. It would certainly include:

- The do-anything service of a West Coast lady who will

feed your pets, handle your shopping, find you an old double-decker London bus, or supplement your fund-raising drive by furnishing a coterie of doorbell ringers.

■ The enterprising artists who do paintings by the square foot. They will cover any wall to order or sculpt to fill any given table space.

■ The firm that packages offbeat, low-cost hiking tours and group vacations to unusual lands where the food might not qualify as haute cuisine but the surroundings furnish material for tall tales back home.

■ The man who creates wall posters to be sold as tourist novelties in different localities. "We mass-produce some without regard to the locality," he grins. "One is a poster giving recipes for local drinks. Most drinks are 'local' to every locality."

Via franchise, you can go into any business from hamburger castles to crime prevention and protection. A recent franchising section in a national newspaper listed these possibilities: postage centers; security systems; sandwiches, ranging from hamburgers to fishburgers, and from hot dogs to hot salami; fashion boutiques; time recording devices; personnel consulting; wig tepees; pollution control devices; financial planning advisory services; garden centers; car washes (you can choose between the regular kind that are set in concrete and go-to-the-customer mobile units); photo centers; steak sit-down restaurants and chicken take-outs; tax systems; mini-cinemas; pizza palazzos; haberdasheries; auto supplies; beauty salons; antique shops; travel agencies; muffler centers; dry cleaners and wet coin-op laundries; agencies to sell counterfeit-currency detection devices; find-a-car aids; insurance centers; kid care nurseries; rental headquarters; temporary help agencies; data processing; auto auctioneering agencies; transmission repair shops; art studios; brake centers; tune-up shops. The franchising world is wide indeed.

One observer has stated that payroll complexities, tax forms, labor laws, and other business complications of the latter part of the twentieth century have made self businesses difficult. "But," he noted, "franchising is changing all that and bringing entrepreneurs back to small business."

To help with franchising, the Small Business Administration has a publication, Management Development Program on Franchising (available from Superintendent of Documents, Government Printing Office, Washington, D.C., at $1.25). It defines franchising this way:

> In the more commonly understood sense, franchising is taken to mean the licensing of an individual to conduct a specific type of business according to a predetermined pattern developed and perfected by the franchisor.
>
> The franchised establishments which operate within a particular franchise system are usually identified as members of a group. They operate under a common trade name—for example, Chicken Delight, Dunkin' Donuts, MacDonald's, and so on. Their business operation, their establishment's appearance, their merchandise—even their operating procedures are standardized to a very high degree. In their efforts to maintain a standardized image and marketing approach to the general buying public, the franchisors usually retain a strong, formalized system of control of the business operation. In this type of franchise, the responsibilities of both parties—franchisor and franchisee—are spelled out in the franchise contract, and are usually considered to be of mutual advantage to both parties.

These contracts are easy to start, harder to drop. Before plumping down cash for a crime detection agency because you believe in tighter enforcement or buying a car wash franchise out of fastidiousness, you should understand that there is more to choice of a franchise than merely selecting a field you like. Notes the Small Business Administration study:

> The franchise system may be used for either goods or services. Although most franchise businesses are in consumer lines, some involve industrial goods and services. In any case, however, they work in generally the same manner. The purchaser of the franchise—the franchisee—is an independent businessman who contracts for a "package" business. Normally, this contract obligates the businessman to some combination of the following:
> 1. To make a minimum investment of money.
> 2. To obtain and maintain a standardized inventory and/or equipment package.

3. To maintain a specified quality level of performance.

4. To follow specified operating procedures and the promotional efforts of the parent firm.

5. To pay royalty or franchise fees.

6. To engage in a continuing business relationship.

While this may seem excessively binding upon the franchisee, the franchise contract usually puts a similar responsibility on the franchisor. The franchisor usually guarantees the franchisee some combination of these elements:

1. Use of the company name.

2. Use of identifying symbols, designs, and facilities.

3. Professional management and employee training.

4. Wholesale prices on specific merchandise.

5. Financial assistance (of various types).

6. Continuing aid and guidance.

The parent company earns its money through the continuing success of its franchises. For this reason, franchisors constantly continue to assist their franchisees with training, promotion, advertising, and new product development, and generally assist with any problems that crop up.

The franchisee has the advantage of a "proven" business formula, and is literally led by the hand to success in his venture.

Typically, a franchisee (that's you; the company selling franchises is called a franchisor) works long hours and seldom enjoys extended weekends at the seaside—certainly not in his initial years. There are other disadvantages. The SBA study spelled them out this way:

> The franchisee . . . must share the income from the business in some manner with the franchisor, whether in the form of a percent of gross sales, a markup on supplies, a flat annual fee, or a combination of these.
>
> He must also accept a certain amount of control over his method of operation, agree to handle a product or products that may not be particularly profitable in his marketing area, or otherwise be subject to certain policies and business practices that benefit others in the chain, but may be injurious to him.

Many big-city daily papers' advertising columns list franchise offerings. They are also found in financial journals and trade publications. Some cities have annual franchise exhibitions. Two directories list franchising companies; these are *The Franchise Annual*, published by National Franchise Reports, 333 N. Michigan Ave., Chicago, Ill., and *Directory of Franchising Organizations and a Guide to Franchising*, put out by Pilot Industries, Inc., 42 W. 33rd St., New York, N.Y.

Whether you decide on a franchised deal or go it alone for the potentially higher profits and possibly greater satisfaction of personal accomplishment, there are factors to be considered. One of these is the matter of raising money. Chapter Two has suggestions on capital sources.

Where Can You Learn
Business Operation?

If you decide upon a franchise, help—as they said in old movies about the French Foreign Legion—is on the way. It comes from the franchisor with whom you deal and whose products or services you sell. The quality will vary with the ability of the franchising company.

It is more difficult when your option was for individual entrepreneurship. Even here, help can be summoned. One of the sources is the ubiquitous Small Business Administration, which we have quoted extensively. It offers such publications, aids, pamphlets, and broadsides as these:

An Employee Suggestion System for Small Companies
One Hundred and Fifty Questions for a Prospective Manufacturer
Human Relations in Small Industry
Improving Materials Handling in Small Plants
Public Accounting Services for Small Manufacturers
Cutting Office Costs in Small Plants
Better Communications in Small Business
Making Your Sales Figures Talk
Cost Accounting for Small Manufacturers
Design Is Your Business
Sales Training for the Smaller Manufacturer
Executive Development in Small Business

The Small Manufacturer and His Specialized Staff
The Foreman in Small Industry
A Handbook of Small Business Finance
Health Maintenance Programs for Small Business
New Product Introduction for Small Business Owners
Profitable Advertising
Technology and Your New Products
Ratio Analysis for Small Business
Profitable Small Plant Layout
Practical Business Use of Government Statistics
Research Relations between Engineering Educational Institutions and Industrial Organizations
Guides for Profit Planning
Personnel Management Guides for Small Business
Profitable Community Relations for Small Business
Small Business and Government Research and Development
Management Audit for Small Manufacturers
Insurance and Risk Management for Small Business
Management Audit for Small Retailers
Financial Recordkeeping for Small Stores
Small Store Planning for Growth
Selecting Advertising Media—A Guide for Small Business
Starting and Managing a Small Business of Your Own
Starting and Managing a Small Credit Bureau and Collection Service
Starting and Managing a Service Station
Starting and Managing a Small Bookkeeping Service
Starting and Managing a Small Building Business
Starting and Managing an Aviation Fixed Base Operation
Starting and Managing a Small Motel
Starting and Managing a Small Duplicating and Mailing Service
Starting and Managing a Small Restaurant
Starting and Managing a Small Retail Hardware Store
Starting and Managing a Small Retail Drugstore
Starting and Managing a Small Dry Cleaning Business
Starting and Managing a Small Automatic Vending Business
Starting and Managing a Carwash

Starting and Managing a Swap Shop or Consignment Sale Shop

Starting and Managing a Small Shoe Service Shop

I talked recently to a friend who is dean of a college of business administration. "We're here," he told me, "to teach business. Most students take a four-year course and a great number go on to achieve MBA degrees. But the man or woman interested in any single specialized field of business knowledge should look into what the university offers. We have many who 'audit,' that is, they take the courses without examination and without credit. In addition, the university's evening division offers specialized business education not aimed at undergraduates but at the kind of person likely to be starting a new business. These are succinct, practical, and usually taught by people from the field rather than by the faculty."

The manufacturer or wholesaler who supplies your merchandise can also be a source of counseling and training. He has a stake in your success. If the field you plan to enter has a trade association, get in touch with its secretary. Many offer how-to courses.

NINE QUESTIONS:

Q. *Would it be better to buy a going business rather than start from scratch?*

A. Harry Sandoval, Jr., Administrator of the Small Business Administration, has pointed out that "in some ways, the person who buys a going business has an advantage over the one who starts from scratch. . . . He has more facts to work with—*if* he knows where to find them and how to use them."

Mr. Sandoval's *if* is the key word in that quotation.

Before buying a business, make sure you aren't taking on someone else's troubles instead of an inflation hedge and profit maker. Search for accurate answers to questions like these: Is the sales territory going down? Am I paying too much for good will? Do the selling owner's methods of accounting truy reflect a picture of the company's profitability? Is the price right in relation both to past profits and to the profits I can reasonably expect it to generate under new management?

Q. *Could business costs be cut by use of temporary help agencies?*

A. Workers supplied by a temporary help service are quickly available. Experienced and well qualified, they need little, if any, breaking in—they can usually walk in and begin to function right away. By using workers from this source you can adjust to fast-breaking opportunities or problems without interrupting your regular schedule. BUT—

In some instances the disadvantages may involve answering complaints of regular employees who lose overtime work because of the temporary workers. It is possible a change of personnel may occur during the assignment. The work itself may mean that temporary help cannot be used as effectively as regular employees.

Temporary help usually costs more on an hourly, daily, or weekly basis than regular employees would be paid. This is offset, however, by avoidance of fringe benefits.

Q. *Is it a good idea to turn a hobby into a business?*

A. That depends upon the hobby—and you. The same considerations apply here as in choosing any business to beat inflation. If the field is overcrowded, you should think a long time about going into it no matter how much fun it might be and regardless of the expertise you already possess. If it is one with wide profit opportunities, a hobby can make an ideal business. Analyze profits, not pleasure opportunity.

Q. *Will I need the help of a CPA, or can an ordinary, garden type of bookkeeping knowledge serve me?*

A. For daily bookkeeping, you shouldn't need a certified public accountant. To audit the company (and possibly to help you set up a meaningful daily plan), the CPA is a handy guy.

On this subject, B. LaSalle Woelful, CPA, of Southern Illinois University, Carbondale, had this to say:

> In providing a professional opinion about the fairness of a company's financial statements, financial audits help to show up weaknesses in management. Thus they are a tool which owner-managers can use for locating and correcting problems in their small companies. . . . Such an examination of a company's financial records focuses attention on areas which require management improvement.

Q. *Some franchising companies' accounting methods have been under fire. Does this mean I might by gypped?*

A. Gyps can arise in any field. Considering its fast growth and the newness of mass franchising as a distribution method, remarkably few shady methods are observable. The practices under fire have more to do with picture painting for stockholders and investors than with franchisee relations. Some franchising firms have taken into immediate current income the franchising fees as soon as a franchisee signs up, even though the total fee may not be paid out for a lengthy time. The accounting profession feels that this inaccurately inflates earnings.

Q. *Are there bad practices I should watch for in buying a franchise?*

A. The SBA study on franchising has suggested that prospective franchisees should walk wide of franchisors "Who grossly exaggerate potential earnings. . . . Whose costs for equipment and supplies are outrageously high. . . . Whose royalty and other financing charges are exorbitantly out of proportion to sales volume. . . . Who have a record of business failures. . . . Whose selection of new sites is haphazard."

Q. *Where would I go for entirely new ideas?*

A. The more you innovate, the more your potential reward may increase, *but* the more your risk increases as well. If you accept the added risks of stepping off established paths into unmapped marketing areas, you might consider patents. All patents are public records. Moreover, many corporations with large research and development departments find that research efforts sometimes result in products which are interesting and useful but completely outside a company's merchandising talents. Such patents are frequently put on sale to outsiders.

Q. *Why didn't you mention mail order as a kind of business?*

A. Because it is not a kind of business. It is a selling method. Many products have been moved successfully by mail and it is a relatively easy break-in for sideline business operators.

Q. *What qualities should I consider in a prospective business partner?*

A. First, integrity.

Next, a personality with which you can work smoothly in double harness.

Partnerships work well when two people with different skills, both needed in the business, can put those skills together harmoniously. Or when one party has the skill and contacts within a field and the other has the necessary funds for financing the venture.

11

Meanwhile, Back
at the Ranch

THIS CHAPTER WILL DETAIL WAYS you can beat inflation on the home front. It will go into methods for obtaining more—and occasionally better—merchandise at less cost. It will examine ideas for cutting the food bill, the new car bill, bank charges and interest payments, and the costs of clothing, education, appliances, and furniture. It will set out ideas for avoiding wastage around the home.

Here J. J., A. A., and K. K., old cowhand cattlemen from an earlier chapter, ride once more.

This time, they do so in the persons of their granddaughters, Jill Jackie, Alice Abigail, and Kathy Karen, station wagon riders of a big-city suburb and wives of middle-income husbands who have a hard time keeping pace with inflation's bite into the ever-lessening dollar.

The place is Alice's kitchen. Coffee steams in three cups. The housewives have jointly shopped local stores and jointly found an increasing number of things getting out of reach which they could once routinely afford.

"Among ourselves we should be able to do something on the suburban ranch-style home front," said Kathy, stirring in an extra teaspoonful of sugar substitute. "Any ideas, J. J.?"

"Around my family," said Jill, "we have been in the position of the old fellow in a cartoon who asked, 'How come there's so much of the month left when the money goes?' That is, until we set up a plan."

How to Make and Maintain a Budget

"Budget? Is that what you mean?" asked A. A. "Trash. I've done it dozens of times. Budgeting doesn't work."

"You sound like your hidebound old grandpop back on the the Western range, A. A.," said J. J. "He isn't too receptive to new ideas, as I remember. Always squinting up at that blamed sky. Unless we want to ride off into our own brand of sunset, we had better be more alert than those cowhands ever were. There is a reason your budgeting didn't work. Most budgeting fails because people take *a* budget out of some book which says that, given so many children, so much income, and so much tax base, certain percentages must go to food, rent, and the like. That is nonsense. A budget has to be individual."

On this professionals in the difficult field of family planning agree with J. J. A budget won't work unless it is made expressly for you. Wrote Betty S. Martin, Director of the Women's Division of the Institute of Life Insurance, in a March 1966 study entitled *A Discussion of Family Money; How Budgets Work and What They Do:*

> There is no such thing as an "average" allowance for a ten-year-old child or an "average" food expenditure for your particular family. This does not mean that spending habits of people in this country aren't being continually studied, or that all kinds of "model" and "average" and "standard" and "minimum" systems for allocating family money are not found in

your library or in the newspapers and magazines. It simply means that however interesting these systems may be, not one of them is likely to be a measuring rod you can use for your family.

The essence of money management is to work out your own plan, one which you and your family have set up together and are satisfied with.

Although prearranged percentage-of-income budgets won't work for every family (and may not work for any family), the same items appear on everyone's budget. And a budget, whether called that or known as an "allocation," a "family plan," or "that-nutty-thing-we-set-up-last-December," is necessary if you are going to fight inflation effectively back home. Here is a suggested form (Figure 4) given by the U.S. Department of Agriculture in *A Guide to Budgeting* (Home and Garden Bulletin 98):

RECORD OF OUR EXPENSES

Date	Item (or service) bought	Classified as—			Gifts and contributions
		Food and beverages	Shelter	Household operation	
		$	$	$	$
Total		$	$	$	$

FIGURE 4

The USDA's Bulletin on budgeting suggests that you follow certain steps:

1. Estimate income for the period ahead.

2. Estimate fixed expenses. These are the things that often can't be altered. They include rent or mortgage, utility bills, and existing installment debts (more later on how to cut costs of future installment purchases).

3. Enter flexible expenses. These are the things you can cut out, cut down, alter, or change. Examples are food and beverage costs, personal allowances, and department store purchases.

4. Compare income and expenses. "That's where we went off," wailed Alice. "There was too much outgo to balance income. I'm like that old cartoon fella—a lot of the month left after the money goes. Inflation makes it worse all the time."

5. Settle upon a workable balance. "Easier said than carried out," said K. K. "But I agree, we have to do it. Either that or move back on the range with your two old cowhand ancestors. Maybe we could subsist by rustling steaks out there. Don't know where we'd get mushrooms to put on the filets, though."

6. Make the plan work. "Ouch," said J. J., A. A., and K. K. in unison. "This won't be pleasant."

The ladies were right. Budgeting is not always pleasant. But it need not be unpleasant. The savings it can bring about become a weapon in overcoming the erosion that income dollars undergo before they become expense payments. Most authorities agree that, for a budget to work, it should not be inflexible even if it is custom tailored. Says the Department of Agriculture Advisory bulletin: "At the end of the budget period, compare what you actually spent with what you planned to spend. . . . If your first plan didn't work in all respects, you shouldn't be discouraged. A budget is not a 'one shot deal,' something you make once and never touch again. Instead, you keep reworking a budget until it works for you and the results satisfy you."

"If this planning is going to satisfy any of us," said J. J., "we must get specific. Let's look at some of the places we can save money so an anti-inflation budget will work. And let's have more of that delicious coffee, A. A. My cup runneth dry."

Savings from the Supermarket

Food cost savings can begin before you ever reach the supermarket. "My Fred has turned suburban farmer on weekends," reported Kathy. "Have you seen the peapod patch back of our rancho? He is growing five different kinds of vegetables. They taste delicious when you pick them out of the garden and pop them into the pot—and they are a great deal cheaper than the kind on the market's produce self. The kids get a bang out of this, too. My oldest insists on wearing a big-brimmed farmer hat when he goes out to dig carrots."

For maximum savings, a garden like this should be planned to furnish the vegetables which will be highest in price at the time they mature. "Fred says there is no use planting what's cheap anyway," continued K. K. "He's in it for the saving, not to dig the good earth."

Figures from the U.S. Department of Agriculture indicate that only 39 cents of the average food dollar in 1968 went to pay farmers. So the closer you can crowd your marketing to the farmer, the greater the savings can be, because the 61 cents of processing, transportation, middleman, and instantizing costs which are partially eliminated are the big end of the checkout tab.

Many cities have farmers' markets where suppliers from the surrounding countryside sell to consumers direct from the truck tailgate. People frequently buy higher quality at lower cost this way. "Let's band together," said A. A. "Among the three of us, we should be able to buy in fairly large quantity. Sharing it three ways, we can have variety yet not have to purchase so much our individual freezers will overflow."

In buying any kind of freezer food, you need a knowledge of grades. Says the U.S. Department of Agriculture in a helpful advisory, *How to Buy Meat for Your Freezer* (Home and Garden Bulletin No. 166, April 1969):

> The shield-shaped USDA grade mark is a guide to the quality of meat—its tenderness, juiciness and flavor—while the round inspection mark is an assurance of wholesomeness. . . . USDA meat grades, such as U.S. Prime, U.S. Choice, U.S. Good, are based on nationally uniform Federal standards of quality. . . . You can be sure that a U.S. Choice rib roast, for example, will provide the same good eating no matter where or when you buy it.

While more expensive grades cost more, cheaper meats usually have equal nutritional value. In such dishes as hamburger and meat loaf, they can barely be distinguished from expensive meats. Whatever the grade, you need to know how it will cut, for if you buy too many cuts your family won't eat, the saving will vanish as surely as if the freezer door stood open for meat to spoil (see Figures 5, 6, and 7).

"Hey, girls, I ran across something last summer that can help us all," said J. J. suddenly. "All my life I believed that epicurean dishes had to be made with meat. Top-grade dining

LAMB CHART

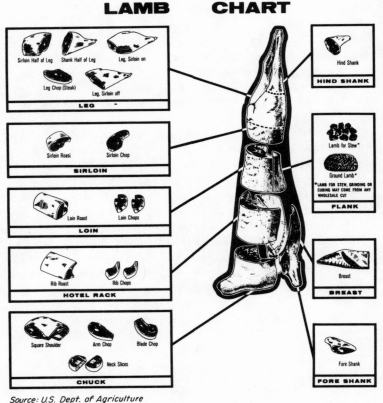

Source: U.S. Dept. of Agriculture

FIGURE 5

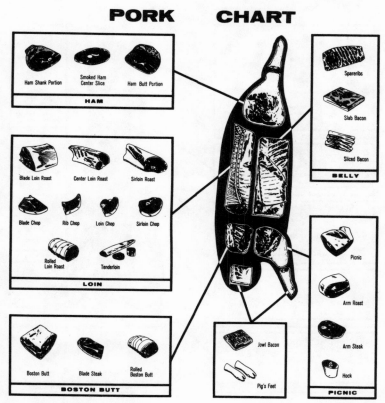

Source: U.S. Dept. of Agriculture

FIGURE 6

out meant filet mignon or sirloin. Then we took a trip to San Francisco—you can eat well there—and learned that its people put seafood higher on the gourmet list than meat. So do many in New Orleans, another stronghold against taste mediocrity.

"Cheeses, eggs, and other foods that have a lot of protein will fill in for meat. Let me send you recipes I've been using. Eggs sardou, eggs soufflé au gratin, or a creole omelet make even my steak-minded husband happy."

Before leaving the supermarket, you—along with J. J., A. A., and K. K., our riders of the suburban sagebrush—should visit

BEEF CHART

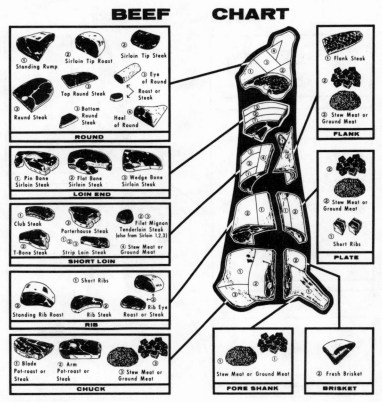

Source: U.S. Dept. of Agriculture

FIGURE 7

nonfood departments. "Nothing new about that idea," said Kathy Karen. "I've been buying routine drugs like aspirin, along with toothpaste and other staples, in the market's drug department. It saves as much as $25.00 a month. That's $300.00 a year."

Save Money When You Shop Downtown

Jill closed her purse as the three housewives walked from a downtown parking lot where they had stabled A. A.'s family station wagon. "Walter and I worked out some ideas for saving money on clothing, hard goods, and other things that make our department store bills so high each month. Let me tell you about some of the ideas while we walk," she said.

1. *Don't Let a Dealer Nail Merchandise to the Floor* "Nailing merchandise to the floor" works this way.

A. A., J. J., and K. K. have been attracted by an advertisement for—wonder of wonders—an electric dryer at $25.00. Joyously, they troop to the sales floor, where they are shown the advertised item. All three are ready to say "charge it" when the salesman holds up a hand.

"That wreck? You don't want it in your homes, ladies. Why, it has at least ten faults which I will enumerate. But this model over here at only $250.00 . . ."

If you have ever been up-sold from an advertised special to a routinely expensive competitive product, you know the pitch. Don't fall for it. If the item advertised is a true bargain, you have a right to buy it. Few stores will outright refuse to sell an advertised special. If one does, you can threaten action with Better Business Bureaus and other guardians of the public's purse and the business community's conscience.

2. *Buy at Sales, But Not All Sales* "Do you know the difference between something advertised as a $5.00 'value' and an item advertised as 'regularly $5.00'?" asked J. J. "One is likely to be a special purchase. The other is almost always an item which in truth sold for $5.00 as a regular price before being marked down."

End-of-season clearance sales nearly always feature the true mark-down bargain. But even in these, special purchases of an inflated "value" are occasionally included. Sales held during the height of a season, as before Christmas instead of after it, are likely to feature special purchases more than marked-down regular merchandise.

"My husband, Walter, is purchasing agent for his company," said J. J. "He says that when you can get real distress merchandise, then you obtain the best bargains. Merchandise is in 'distress' when it has to be sold because a season is ending or a shelf is too full, tying up capital in slow sellers."

3. Shop the Offbeat Stores   Those who routinely check prices in discount stores frequently find that savings permit them to live higher on their inflation-eroded dollars than can friends who shop only the conventional outlets.

People who shop this way say, however, that there are drawbacks as well as disadvantages.

"You have to put out money for a whole month's purchases to make any savings meaningful," J. J. continued. "And you miss the delivery, personal service, and long hours of regular retailers."

Discount stores sell all kinds of merchandise. Nationally advertised brands of clothing are sometimes obtainable at 25 percent off, but there are no alteration services (and, in most cases, no provisions for returns except on obviously defective merchandise). Yet here, too, the saving can be worth the risk. A. A. interposed: "Bert looks like a millionaire in $125.00 suits costing $75.00, and we pay about $5.00 to $6.00 to a tailor for alterations."

Discounters sell all kinds of merchandise. A shopper has to be careful to see that he has indeed bought $125.00 worth for $75.00. Some unscrupulous outfitters are not above bringing in $25.00 merchandise to sell for $75.00. Yet from reputable firms it is possible to buy a lot for less and live richer without a higher income. Orthodox retailers, such as department stores, offer periodic sales, shaving the list prices while still giving regular service such as charges and alterations.

4. Don't Accept Lemons   Some kind of warranty is implied in every sale, but the best stores give adjustments and offer returns and credit purchase prices in excess of their legal obligations to customers. "Walter insists we buy only from the reputable firms that take back lemon merchandise," said J. J. "He says any saving on ten bargain purchases can be wiped out by the loss on one refusal to adjust for a bad piece of merchandise."

Where a firm's people say, "Sorry, no returns," you might still have recourse short of an expensive and time-consuming lawsuit. In every organization there are many with authority to say "no" but few—sometimes only one—with authority to say "yes" to a demand. He is usually the boss. Being boss, he cares about the attitude of customers from a longer-term viewpoint than a single sale. "Walter bought a shirt last week that came apart at the seams first time I ran it through the washer," J. J. told her friends. "When he was told, 'Sorry—no money back on sale merchandise,' my husband mailed the shirt to the store president. A few days later he received an apology and a credit."

5. *Avoid High Interest Charges on Your Purchases*   Big banks offer credit cards good at stores, restaurants, everywhere, from beauty salons to barrooms. It's a temptation to run up high bills because the banks will allow customers to take many months paying such charges.

"Why not?" shrugged a bank vice-president to whom I brought this up. "We're charging $1\frac{1}{2}$ percent a month on balances older than 25 days. That's 18 percent interest a year. We can't get 18 percent on many types of lending."

"Such a whopping interest might be good from his standpoint, but not from ours," Jill pointed out as the housewives moved to a second store. "Walter can make a straight loan at lower interest if we need the money. No use letting 18 percent be added to the cost of things."

6. *Brand or Offbrand Merchandise?*   You have to determine this item by item. Some retailers' house brands are better made and sell at lower markup than nationally advertised brands. There are other times when a national brand's known quality represents a truer bargain than an off brand at a claimed special saving.

"The point," said J. J., "is to do what our grandfathers back on the Western range would do—know the brands. And the off brands."

Pay Less, Get More, When You Buy a Car

"Hottest thing around. Performance? This car has got it. And everything else."

Automobile salesmen are enthusiastic men. They have to be in their competitive field. And so statements like that can sometimes be heard when you shop for a new car. Don't believe such a claim—or disbelieve it either—without asking the salesman to show you something called "Performance Data for New Cars and Motorcycles." It is put out by the U.S. Department of Transportation. Secretary of Transportation John Volpe has described it as "the finest consumer information package in automotive history." According to the Secretary's office,

> Manufacturers are . . . required to provide a booklet for each new car, either as an individual publication or as part of the owner's manual. . . . The information covers three specific areas: Stopping ability, acceleration and passing; and tire reserve load. . . . A number of additional performance categories are under consideration, including side door strength and driver's field of view.

Don't be fooled into believing that pricing of cars is uniform. It is not the same even between dealers selling the same model with identical window stickers. The automobile industry, and its sideline the truck industry, are still in the Oriental bazaar period of merchandising where the price a customer pays—even if he is buying a fleet—is set by haggling, and nobody knows whether he got a good deal or whether some sharper-minded, tougher-bargaining fellow who came after him got an even better one. You will be ahead if you check out certain points before you say, "Okay, I'll take it."

■ *How much,* NET, *for the new vehicle?* At the time this is written, the auto manufacturers' window sticker lists are under governmental scrutiny. Items that the window lists are all there on the car. But the numbers don't mean a great deal.

Recently, a friend of mine priced a medium-range car. Those

with the features he wanted carried "list" prices of about $4,400.00. He offered a two-year-old car in trade. The dealer agreed to sell for $2,700. "You're saying that my two-year-old car is worth $1,700 in trade?" my friend asked in amazement.

"Not at all," the auto salesman replied. "We'll resell your car for about $800.00. I'd sell the car to you at about $3,500.00 whether you had a trade-in or not."

Keep in mind that auto buying is a haggling business. Resist efforts to use the window stickers as a comparison of value. Instead, ask: "Here's what I want. There is my trade-in. How much cash difference do you want?"

■ *What tires come with the car?* If one company offers a car with lower-grade tires, while from another you can obtain more expensive substitutions and both vehicles sell at the same net figure for old car plus cash, you obviously receive higher value from the seller who furnishes the safer, longer-wearing tires. A fleet operator figures that the original-equipment tires on new cars are good for no more than 12,000 to 15,000 miles, while good replacement tires will roll 20,000 to 25,000 miles.

■ *How many dealers have you shopped?* "A Ford is a Ford, given the same number of features and extras," one executive claimed when I asked this question. I told him about my own recent purchase of a Mustang. We wanted power steering, automatic transmission, air conditioning, and radio. Three dealers were visited. The high dealer was approximately $400.00 above the lowest dealer. The percentage difference was about 17 percent.

Unless you are so sold on a Ford—used here only as an example—that no other car would be considered, it also pays to shop for competing cars. While the low-bidding Ford dealer was $400.00 under his higher-priced colleague, a Camaro, Chevrolet's direct competitor to the Mustang, could have been had at an additional saving of nearly $100.00.

Moreover, the price lines of car brands tend to blur into each other. There are Buicks competitive with some of the models put out by Ford, Chevrolet, Dodge, or Plymouth. Oldsmobile makes models in the Cadillac range. Pontiac might have something competitive with Mercury.

The idea is to make sure that Friendly Old Car Dealer Ferd isn't giving you a friendly old snow job because he looks on you as a customer of whom he is sure.

■ *Have you checked dealers in other communities?* Sometimes the small-town or suburban dealer can give a better price than the big-city shop. If he has had to order X number of cars and just can't peddle that many to the natives, he is likely to go courting city folks to work off inventory. On the other hand, small-town residents sometimes find that the bargains are in the showrooms and on the lots of big-city dealerships. There is no one right way to do this. But it is smart to shop the other half of the world to see what it offers when you buy an item as big-ticket as a car.

■ *How good is the dealer's service?* Excellence or incompetence of service—how much is warranty, how much pay work, its speed or snail-like slowness—won't look as big in the cost picture as the immediate price you pay for a vehicle. But it can affect ultimate cost.

"It's not the five minutes the mechanic needs to make an adjustment," fumed one owner after his vehicle had been in a service shop for days, "it is the five days it takes him to get around to the adjustment."

The above is not intended as a slur upon car dealers' service in general or the service offered by independent shops. But it is a fact that downtime adds to a vehicle's cost. You will be well advised to check dealer reputation for speed as well as for reliability of service.

Lower the Cost of Education

Once, $500 per year saw you comfortably through college. The cost of education has soared considerably since that prewar day. Now it might take from four to eight times as much to put a son or daughter through a university.

There are ways to cut that cost. All involve borrowing. Before throwing up your hands and saying that the money must be paid back anyway, so what's the use of adding interest costs to already high tuition charges, you should know the following:

■ Given a continuing inflation, which is the premise on which we're working, you or your youngster after he finishes school will pay back cheaper, easier-to accumulate dollars.

■ Many of the loans are at smaller interest than the rate at which you could borrow comparable amounts through orthodox channels.

■ Some loans bear no interest until a given period after graduation.

■ Some loans carry no interest charges at all.

Many loan programs are federally financed. The terms of these are subject to change (but won't be changed once you sign up). Some apply only to low-income groups. Others scale the benefits up to middle-income families. Universities offer their own financial-aid systems. At some colleges (my own is one) alumni-financed scholarships are available.

Find out which programs apply in your case and at the college of your child's choice by asking the university.

Health Care Needn't Break Your Budget

For most of us not eligible for Medicare or Medicaid, the only way to avoid the financial disaster which can come with extended sickness is through health care insurance. Some policies cover your needs superbly; others spread only a scant blanket over the disabled. Whether to plump down cash for one kind of policy or another should be discussed with an insurance expert. When you talk to him, you bring up these questions about health care coverage:

■ *Group policy or an individualized one?* Sometimes, the group policy comes with a job and you buy it willy-nilly. Other times it is an optional matter, as when you belong to a club or organization which offers policies to members but does not demand that members buy.

Group policies usually cost less. But their provisions may not be the ones which you require. An individual policy can be custom-designed, but, like anything else custom-made, it is likely to be higher in cost. Some people compromise by taking the group policy, then add outside individualized coverage for extra frills or protections.

It is well to know that no coverage is better than the company offering it. Choose a sound, well-known company. Keep in mind the example of the admittedly far-out, but still real, case of a mail-order life insurance company—now itself defunct—whose policies provided that benefits could be paid only if the deceased appeared in person to make a claim five days after death.

■ *Is maternity covered?* Some health care policies specifically exclude maternity care, or else put such a low dollar limit on the payments that it might as well be excluded. Yet maternity confinement is the hospitalization most likely to be needed during a family's young and middle years.

■ *Do benefits apply immediately?* Alice had an automobile accident only three days after being accepted for a health care policy. Prolonged, painful back surgery was needed. "At least," she said to Bert, "the family's bank account won't be crippled. Even surgeon's fees are taken care of by the new policy." Both were shocked when the agent apologetically pointed out that the policy excluded coverage until thirty days after date of issuance.

■ *Does the policy cover follow-up treatment?* After that happy day when you leave a hospital there sometimes remains long and often expensive treatment in the physician's office or hospital clinics. Some health care policies provide for follow-up treatment. Others exclude it. As a general thing you will have to pay a higher premium to secure the coverage; whether to do so is a personal decision.

■ *Are surgical-medical fees part of the policy?* Here, too, you will pay more to get the fee coverage. If you buy such coverage, read the fine print carefully. Discover whether the fees to be paid out are realistic or are based upon those charged by doctors back when Hippocrates was the medical light of ancient Greece. Is fee coverage purely surgical, or is your regular doctor's attendance also to be reimbursed by the company? Learn whether nursing care—outside as well as in the hospital —is covered.

One young woman learned the painful way to look for such

extras. When a smashup broke both of her arms, she suffered additional face damage for which a dental specialist had to be called.

"Nope," said the claim adjuster when she presented his bill. "Your policy calls for payment to medical doctors. The dentist has to be on you."

■ *Is disability coverage enough?* It is not many years since a convalescent could live adequately on $75.00 per week. The progress of inflation has been steady since then. Disability payments have to be realistic in view of the cost of living while disabled.

■ *Are premium payments suspended upon disability?* "No use giving it out to a policyholder with one hand while taking it partially back with the other," an insurance agent explained to Alice and Bert. "Unless a policy calls for suspension of payments to the company during the disability period, a policyholder's payments are lessened by the amount he has to continue giving to the company."

■ *How many exclusions?* Many policies will not pay for treatment of certain diseases or disabilities and limit the amounts to be paid on others. Generally, you should look for a policy with the fewest exclusions, the widest latitude. "Why gamble on what *kind* of disease you might have, when the purpose of health care is to take care of all financial risk?" said A. A. to her friends when she returned from the hospital stay.

Save around the Ranch

"Say, girls," said K. K. when they met for coffee after their downtown trip. "I worked out a way to save on costs for service. Fred's family lives out in the Middle West and we wanted to send back pictures of the children. A regular in-town studio quoted $152, which at the moment was more than we could shell out no matter how professional their work. So I called the job reference bureau on the campus.

" 'Anybody interested in some portrait work for a recent grad?' I asked—and out came a journalism major who did a job few pros could have matched. Now when we need any sort of odd services which students perform, I call the college.

This provides useful employment to students who need it and we benefit by services young people on our income can't always afford."

Interested in buying a house? It might pay to look at something bigger than you need—then build an apartment in it (provided local zoning laws allow this). The income received from rental frequently meets 80 percent of the mortgage notes and allows extra income for buying the goodies of life now instead of waiting. Some families find that a regular two-family dwelling gives them all of the privacy they need, plus enough rent to meet the whole monthly note, and they are thus enabled to spend on furnishings what their friends scrimp to put into occupancy costs.

If you are the handy-about-the-house type who can do things with tools, you will save considerably on upkeep whether you have a multi-family dwelling where rents help to meet the notes or whether you live in lonely splendor in a suburban single or an urban apartment. "Just the other day," said J. J., "Walter built up a set of den bookshelves that would have cost hundreds at a home furnishings store. It's a throwback to the times when those range-rider grandfathers did everything for themselves."

"Bert isn't the handyman type," said A. A., "but we're still able to save because I sew a lot of the girls' clothes. Speaking of that, why don't we sew up a party Saturday night? Bert did pretty well in mutual funds this year—enough to keep us ahead of inflation—and we'll buy the booze to celebrate."

SIX QUESTIONS:

Q. *A friend claims that anyone who pays bills promptly loses money. Can this be correct?*

A. Can be, and is. Having said that, let me qualify it by noting that I don't advocate nonpayment of bills. Just don't pay them earlier than necessary.

The average corporation does this. If an invoice carries a discount notation of 1 percent for cash within ten days, that bill will be paid early because businessmen know that 1 percent for ten days is 36.5 percent a year, and such a return on capital is not to be found easily. But most bills carry no such saving. Where they do not, a bill is usually due in thirty, sometimes in twenty-five days.

"No sense paying in three days what doesn't become overdue until thirty," one corporate treasurer said when I talked to him about this.

"The advantage of paying when due—but not before—is obvious. A business is like a family; it always needs working capital. Why should I sacrifice the use of funds that in aggregate come to a sizable amount each month, and then perhaps end up with a short-term bank loan? Better to pay no interest and use our own money as long as possible."

Such businesslike thinking can be applied to family life. It is like having extra short-term borrowed money on which to live better, but paying no interest to get it.

Q. *If I stop buying convenience foods—admittedly costly in relation to those having less processing in the price—I won't know how to judge qualities or quantities. Is there any easy way to learn?*

A. Write the Superintendent of Documents, Government Printing Office, Washington, D.C., for the folio of booklets collectively titled *How to Buy Food*. This includes *How to* booklets on meat for the freezer, beef steaks, beef roasts, fresh vegetables, fresh fruits, cheddar cheese, dry instant nonfat milk, butter, poultry, and eggs. The booklets go into detail on grading, cuts, quality, and nutrition.

Q. *Isn't the 18 percent interest charges of retailers and credit card issuers usury?*

A. Most states have high allowances on this type of lending. Moreover, some interest limits were raised during the crunching 1969 tight-money binge when all rates soared. In a few states, however, interest charges on overdue retail charges are lower than 18 percent. Wherever you are, it's a high-cost way to obtain money.

Q. *People on a payroll who budget know how much money will come in. What should the self-employed do?*

A. Here is a suggestion in the U.S. Department of Agriculture's *Guide to Budgeting for the Family:*

> When your earnings are irregular, base your estimate on your previous income and current prospects. If your income fluctuates sharply—as it may for seasonal workers, salesmen on commission, farmers and other self-employed people—play it safe by making two estimates. Work out the smallest and the largest figures you can reasonably expect. Plan first on the basis of the low income figure. Then consider how you will use additional amounts.

Q. *Is merchandise in discount stores equal to that at higher prices in conventional outlets?*

A. A nationally advertised name carrying a nationally advertised list price is likely to be the same no matter where you buy it. Not so merchandise billed as identical with the national brand. It may be—but you can't compare the two and be sure of your comparison. Even where national brands sell at different prices in different stores, you'll find occasionally that the cheaper price is for last year's model. It is not bad to buy last year's model. Just know what each price covers.

Q. *Suppose there is only minimal price difference between department store and discount store prices. Where should I shop?*

A. Wherever suits you best. If the discount saving is small, and the added convenience of department stores' charge, adjustment, and delivery services matters to you, then you'd probably do better with the conventional outlet. This is a matter for personal likes and dislikes—as are all suggestions we have covered in this chapter for living well on less money.

12

Form a Price Posse

"ALONE," said Alice, "we are powerless to stop inflation. But if we get together, there is a lot we can do."

"Amen," answered Jill. "That's the way those old grandfathers of ours cleaned up the Wild West a long time ago. Maybe we need to become price vigilantes."

Price Vigilantes

If salaried and self-employed people, doctors, housewives, lawyers, Indian chiefs, cobblers, cake bakers, and all the rest who have suffered so long and silently from this inflationary lessening of our ability to survive should band together as the vigilantes of the Old West banded to put down outlaws, we might be able to halt inflation or render it less damaging. Whenever the American people have strongly *and in force* demanded a thing, they have been at least partly successful in getting that thing done.

(The inevitabilities of cost-push, outlined earlier, make it doubtful that price vigilante action, however vigorous, can completely halt inflation. But it can mitigate the effects, at least for a time, and that is no small gain in the fight to survive inflation. One danger in price posse action is that people's interest dwindles if they achieve initial success; you should be aware of this, and if you and friends follow some of the ideas outlined in this chapter, be ready to endlessly fire new enthusiasm in order to keep the vigilantes vigilant.)

How to Make a Price Posse Function

Groups can do things that individuals could never accomplish. A few years ago I was president of a local financial analysts society. A law potentially hurtful to investment advisors was proposed in the state legislature. Not least of many arguments against this bill was that the proposed regulation would duplicate federal scrutiny. Some of the features would have cast advisors in a false position. I discussed this with a colleague at lunch. He proposed applying to the Senate committee for permission to testify.

"You as an individual and I as another individual?" I inquired. "They won't listen. Here's a better idea. We will put it to the society. If its members decide to condemn the bill, then you and I can appear not as individuals but as representatives of a professional group."

This was done. As a result of testimony that followed, the bill was tabled in committee. Single citizens with apparent axes to grind would not have been listened to as respectfully nor would their views have been a vital factor in influencing legislators that the bill was a bad one and should not become law.

The best way for community price vigilantes to make their voices listened to—and their combined force felt—by business and the governmental officials whose actions so often fuel the inflationary fires is to use group action. "For a posse," shouted J. J., "ride the rascals down!"

"We'll begin at the school," Alice added. "All of us have children there. So do 400 other parents. If we start with the families with whom we are in contact, we can later spread out to other school parent groups, then to existing organizations of a different kind, until we cover the city."

At the next monthly PTA meeting, Jill arose. "What I have to say may be outside the regular purpose of a school parents' organization," she began, "but it is important to all parents' ability to provide for their children. If the suggested action cannot be done by a PTA group, let's form a separate organization, and as soon as routine school business has been concluded, we will adjourn the PTA and re-meet as a price posse. My proposal is this. . . ."

An hour later a quickly organized price posse had formed and determined upon certain steps:

"We will jointly agree to fight every price increase that comes along," K. K. said. "Maybe the merchant whose costs are higher has to up his price. But we are hurt should he do so. If the group refuses to sit still for *any* inflationary increases, perhaps the merchant, along with the distributor, manufacturer, union leader, and everyone else, will give thought to cost cutting instead of price increases. Eventually the high cost-spiral might be rolled back." The posse agreed.

"Our posse possesses three weapons," said J. J. "One is publicity. The second is moral force. The third is a buying strike." Again, the group agreed.

"We will first try moral force when a price goes up," A. A. explained. "If three or four of us call as a group upon every passer of higher prices, show the problem both nationally and locally, and explain the necessity for fighting an increase at its birth before it can grow into a big cost-push able to spawn fresh price increases, then a certain percentage of businessmen will join us.

"For those who don't, we'll use the publicity weapon. In the West, where my grandfather still rides a trail, during the old wild and woolly days the practice was to quickly try male-factors who were caught by a posse. If the judgment was 'guilty,' sentence was speedily carried out. For those days and those ways, nothing but such rough and ready justice would have sufficed. We will hold a public 'trial' of every firm and individual who raises prices. The newspapers, radio stations, and television newsmen will be invited. At first they will come for the novelty news value of a mock trial of price offenders. Later, I hope, they will continue to report our vigilante trials because they will see the merit of the method and the absolute need to do something to mitigate inflation before we all end up carrying a wheelbarrow full of big-bill money when we go to shop for necessities. The second step of publicity will be carried out—but only when moral persuasion fails.

"For the worst cases, we reserve the third step. A buyers' strike on many occasions has brought prices down. It is true that prices have usually gone back up. But that has happened because a group, victorious in its buying strike, later disbanded and there was no one to fight the increase when it was quietly reinstituted."

Can such a posse be effective?

"If you doubt it," said K. K., "you should look to the success of pollution control. For many years, thoughtful people were worried about our air and water resources. Nothing happened —until they organized. Now much is being done to clean up the environment, all because there exists organized demand instead of a few individual voices crying in the wilderness of concrete and carbon monoxide."

Educating the Community

"It's only fittin', as our granddads would say, that this posse should begin in a schoolhouse," said A. A., as the housewives drank coffee next morning in her kitchen, "since much of its job is going to be educational."

To understand the function of educational vigilantism, start with an understanding of crowd psychology. If the public participates in movements outlined by a price posse, the chance for success is high. If the public shrugs its collective shoulder and turns to the comics instead of the pages with grocery prices, then even the best of posse power won't become effective.

Gustave Le Bon, a turn-of-the-century French observer, was possibly the first person to apply scientific methods to the analysis of crowd behavior. His book *The Crowd* is considered a classic by many behavioral scholars.

There are two kinds of crowds, Le Bon noted, and the kind that is of interest to a price posse is called a "psychological" crowd. This type of crowd is not always or necessarily a large group gathered together; scattered dozens who have never seen or heard of each other might constitute a psychological crowd. Crowd pressures, Le Bon noted, will force the denial not only of logic and reason, but, sometimes, of the clear evidence of an individual's own eyes and ears.

In his treatise, Le Bon stated what he called the "law of crowds." A crowd has a "collective mentality which makes them think, feel, and act in a manner quite different from that in which each individual would think, feel, and act were he in a state of isolation." The crowd becomes a "provisional being formed of heterogeneous elements which for a moment are combined, exactly as the cells which constitute a living body form by their reunion a new being which displays characteristics very different from those possessed by each of the cells singly." In crowds (even when widely scattered) the intellectual aptitude of the individual becomes weakened. All this becomes a fact because "the individual forming part of a crowd acquires, solely from numerical considerations, a sentiment of invincible power." Contagion and suggestibility, concluded Le Bon, play a large role in the leaping of ideas from mind to mind in a crowd.

In all times and places certain activities are "in," although what is "in" this year may, through change of public tastes and needs, be "out" in a few years. Currently, it is "in" in almost any community to be a worker for the civic symphony or philharmonic. It can become "in" to belong to the price posse. This fact should be taken into account in snowballing the size of a vigilante group. Moreover, since Le Bon's association-of-ideas psychological observations still apply, the snowballing process will be made more effective if early in the organization's life, names of prominent civic, political, labor union, and business figures are on the list of members.

Group Pressure on Lawmakers

Whether on the state, local, or federal level, officials and bureaucrats look self-righteous when the subject of inflation comes up, and say, "What can *we* do about it?"

In early 1970, it was proposed in Washington that wages and salaries of all federal employees be raised. No one begrudges government employees a slice of the better things— no one fails to recognize that they are sometimes squeezed between higher prices and static salaries. However, those raises were as inflationary as wage raises of teamsters, steelworkers, or corporate presidents and board chairmen.

A few months earlier, the payouts to Social Security recipients had been increased 15 percent. Every year, harried local and state employees demand (and usually get) inflationary across-the-board wage increases. Mayors, governors, and legislators generously dip into the till to increase their personal salaries.

The Posse Must Tell Them to Stop Moreover, wastage in government adds to the need for higher taxes and frequently increases deficit spending, itself a direct cause of monetary inflation.

The Posse Must Tell Them to Stop Governments tend to replace things which do not need replacement and to buy things as status symbols rather than to meet needs. "I counted more IBM electric typewriters in one city office than there were typists to use them," said one disgruntled taxpayer with whom I discussed this.

The Posse Must Tell Them to Stop   Even individuals can do some-thing. Writing in the August–September 1969 issue of *Modern Maturity*, California legislative representatives Ernest Giddings and Peter Hughes told about "Inflation—What You Can Do":

> You, as one individual, may feel that your need and your wishes are never considered. You may be impatient with what seems like neglect by the Congress. You may wonder what you, as one individual, can do.
>
> You can help your own congressman make up his mind. You can help your two United States senators formulate their posi-tion. You can do this by writing three letters.
>
> Each letter can state your specific case or the specific case of a relative or friend. Your letter should be concise, legible, to the point, and on one subject. It should give the member of Con-gress enough information about yourself to identify you as one of his vocal, but concerned constituents. Address your congress-man at the House Office Building, Washington, D.C. 10515, and your senators at the Senate Office Building, Washington, D.C. 20510, and be sure to include your own full address.

Regarding government cost cutting, California Governor Ronald Reagan said in a speech at Knoxville, Tennessee, on October 20, 1969:

> A journalist took me to task recently for saying that nothing was more important than economy in government.
>
> Well, in the last ten years inflation has cost our state more than all the monies spent to build or renovate our schools, or more than all the monies spent for highways, or more than all the monies spent for hospitals and hospital facilities. . . . *I re-peat, nothing is more important right now than economy in government.* . . . unless we do cut the cost of government (so that it begins to live within the means of our taxpayers) we will find ourselves back in the very dark ages—an age of dinosaurs of debt, depression and despair.

Writing to me on December 15, 1969, Caspar W. Wein-berger, Director of Finance of the State of California, pointed out:

Basically, the state has two ways of assisting in the control of inflation. It can take a leadership role in keeping governmental expenditures down—encouraging local restraint as well as achieving economies in the State Budget. Of course, Federal decisions must be in the same direction or state and local restraint will be of no avail. . . . appeals can be made to business and labor to slow the wage/price increases which continue the inflationary spiral.

Congressman Hale Boggs (D-La.), Democratic whip of the U.S. House of Representatives, says this:

As for . . . group efforts to work through government leaders to correct conditions which cause inflation, the most essential effort along these lines would be to let the President know how important it is that he use the immense power of his office to restrain the monopoly powers of business and labor in arriving at wage-price increases which add to the distortions accompanying inflation. . . . Persistent reminders made to government leaders—both in the Executive and Legislative branches—that we must invoke stringent fiscal and monetary restraints to control general price increases would also be helpful.

"We'll buy that," chorused Jill, Alice, and Kathy. "Let the price posse ride to city hall, statehouse—and Washington."

FOUR QUESTIONS:

Q. *What is an ombudsman, and how would he fit into the anti-inflation price posse?*

A. If you have a problem in Sweden—say you want your street repaired and no one at City Hall will send equipment to patch that gaping hole behind the driveway—you can appeal to the ombudsman. If he agrees that public officialdom is at fault, he will see that things get done. He is, in simple definition, a superpower dedicated to help citizens against officialdom.

Q. *New York City has a Department of Consumer Affairs. What does it do? Would such a department work elsewhere?*

A. The traditional ombudsman has jurisdiction over taxpayer and other political affairs. New York's Department of Consumer Affairs is an economic ombudsman. It was set up August 22, 1969. In setting it up, Mayor John V. Lindsay ordered it:

> . . . to investigate the causes of the current inflation, including the extent to which the prices are attributable both to market pressures and to non-market influences of Federal, state and municipal policies; to report the effects of the inflationary cycle on the people of the City of New York; to recommend steps to combat inflation including effective national policies and steps the city can take to remedy the hardships caused by inflation and to urge needed reforms in national policy.

In other words—a price posse. The department has other functions, among them to investigate consumer complaints of all kinds. These often involve inflationary damages. Mayor Lindsay noted in creating the department that "Our city and its people are suffering from rising prices. Cities like New York must assume some responsibility for safeguarding the economic welfare of their citizens. If we do not act, it may be that no one else will."

Q. *Sometimes prices don't go up, but size or quality of merchandise goes down while a price remains seemingly stable. How could a group fight that kind of inflation?*

A. As J. J. shouted at the organizational meeting of her town's price posse: "Ride the rascals down!" People who inflate prices—whether by reducing the size of merchandise or by increasing the size of price tags—are not necessarily rascals. They are frequently victims rather than causes of inflation. But the process must be fought wherever found.

(Few things, truly, are what they seem to be. The "official" size of a standard, seemingly sturdy two-by-four piece of lumber is not, as an observer might expect, two inches by four inches. Recently, the U.S. Department of Commerce announced agreement of a large majority of the industry on the actual minimum size: 1½ inches by 3½ inches dried or 1⁹⁄₁₆ by 3⁹⁄₁₆ inches green. The Secretary of Commerce, according to news reports, hailed this agreement as an "important step for the consumer." He did, however, note that the designation "two-by-four" constituted a problem in nomenclature.)

Q. *How would I—or a local price posse—arrange to testify before a congressional or state legislative committee?*

A. If you go direct to the committee itself, write its chairman, explaining what you want to say and the importancs of having your group's views on record, and respectfully requesting an appointment to appear.

This kind of thing is often best arranged through the congressman from your district (if a U.S. House of Representatives committee is the forum you seek) or one of your senators (if the committee is one of the U.S. Senate). For a state legislative appointment, ask your state senator or representative to smooth the path.

13

Bunkhouse at the End
of the Trail

IT WAS A LATE FALL EVENING. In the living room of A. A.'s
suburban ranch house Jill, Walter, Alice, Bert, Kathy, and
Fred sat talking. Walter waved a glass in the air and started
to speak.

"The time will come," he said, "when we'll all grow older.
We'll be looking for a quiet rest in a bunkhouse at the end
of the trail—is that how your granpa, the trail boss, would put
it, Jill?—and unless we plan carefully, inflation will make the
bunkhouse cost approximately as much in terms of today's
dollars as Buckingham Palace or the Taj Mahal. Inflation
planning has to include what we'll do to make the trail's end
a comfortable place. Let's not be like those who planned for
a retirement scale where $75.00 a month rented a seaside cot-

tage, $2.00 bought a good steak, and the morning newspaper cost a nickel."

Plan Ahead with Inflation in Mind

"If we follow the recommendations in a book called *How You Can Beat Inflation*," mused A. A., "our money at the time of retirement should be mostly in things that grow. We should have achieved some income over the years, using part and plowing back part. Is that the posture to have when we get to the big retirement bunkhouse? In mutual funds, stocks, participations, or real estate that might go on growing but will pay us negligible income? I don't think so. What are the alternatives, group?"

"I believe," said J. J., "that inflation planning has to break down into different phases. In the first, we fight to beat inflation. In the second, we spread out all those goodies we worked so hard to get so we can begin some pleasant retirement years. I want my big bunkhouse to be on the shores of a sea or lake, maybe you want yours in a mountain area, and maybe the best place is right here at home. None of us want it in some penny-pinched third-rate area."

"I talked about this to the company CPA," said Fred. "All he said was, 'Easy. You buy a lot of things that grow. When you retire, you dump them and buy instead some investments that will produce big income. Any dolt can do it.'"

"It would take a dolt to wait until retirement before deciding *how* he was going to make the big years turn into the good years," Walter reflected. "I say, we'll lose it in the end if we don't plan for it now. Where should this thing start?"

Not long ago, an investor put an identical question to me. "I'm not too many years away from retirement," he confided. "I have about $40,000 as a stake. It is presently in bank certificates of deposit whose interest is not keeping me abreast of inflation. When the certificates earn 5 percent, I lose 6 percent to inflation and then another 3 percent to income tax, so that I end behind. What should I do to build this amount if possible—keeping in mind that in a period of years I'll retire and then I will need higher income to offset the salary that will be lost. Should I go in for some gunslinging?"

My advice was: "Invest conservatively.

"Such a stake is not easily replaced in your stage of life," I told him, "—or in any other. For now, use mutual funds or common stocks. Select those with good growth so you'll get ahead of inflation and if possible retire with not only more dollars than you now possess, but more purchasing value as well. Don't worry about dividends. Growth stocks and growth mutuals typically pay less than the staid old income producers. That income, small as it is, will supplement your salary. Income from growth investments tends to get bigger over the years; you should expect small increases.

"Then when you are a year away from retirement, begin *gradually* to shift investments into mutual funds or stocks that will produce greater income albeit with less capital enhancement. Depending upon the money market conditions at the time you retire—it is important to judge these matters close to the retirement date and not decide on the basis of conditions which might be outmoded on your retirement—you might switch to high-income corporate bonds, common stocks of sound companies which pay dependable dividends, if possible with enhancement potential, maybe mutual funds that fit this description. Tax-exempt municipal bonds should be considered, but only if you are in a sufficiently high tax bracket after retirement so that the tax saving will outweigh the slightly smaller return you must accept when you buy bonds of states and municipalities."

The heart of this discussion was an emphasis on capital growth, slowly shifting to income investments, with the precise nature of the income producers to be decided at time of retirement. Such strategy should be set in advance.

While it is relatively easy to move stocks, bonds, and mutual funds from a growth emphasis to concentration on retirement income, a business of your own is a different thing. So are cattle, citrus, petroleum, and other participations. Likewise, a catfish farm, an office building, or a piece of land.

With these, it becomes triply important to plan in advance so you can sell out what you have decided to sell, keep what fits with retirement plans, and be in shape so that when the day of senior-citizen status rolls around, the transition will be smooth and the income sufficient to keep you on the beach in affluence regardless of inflation.

It is unfortunate that I cannot outline a right way to do this. Much depends upon personal preference. Jill likes to keep her hand in with sideline business management; Alice wants to loll beside a resort swimming pool, lazily signalling a waiter to bring lunch and a deck of cards so she can play bridge with friends, doing laps of the pool during the times her hand is dummy. Whether you are Jill or Alice, Walter or Bert, know your preference and work before retirement to make it happen smoothly.

Consider a Withdrawal Plan

Your retirement stake need not be shifted from one form to another. It can be kept as is with the end at which you operate changed on retirement from accumulation to withdrawal. Instead of putting value in, you take it out.

Assume you do this with mutual fund shares. Many funds offer such a plan. You wish to obtain $2,500 every three-month quarter. Your dividends are paid quarterly by the fund but don't equal this amount. The withdrawal plan calls for payment of all dividend amounts, and to make up the full $2,500 amount, the fund will then redeem sufficient shares to bring you up to $2,500.

"We would be eating capital itself if we did things that way," Fred complained when K. K. had proposed they consider a withdrawal plan for eventual retirement. "Sooner or later we would go broke."

"We might," admitted Kathy. "But consider: If inflation gets worse, as we believe it will, and if we have chosen a wisely managed mutual fund to do the withdrawal bit, then enhancement in share values should make up for the dribble of share redemptions needed to put together our $2,500 retirement package. Before long dividends themselves should increase

sufficiently to make up the tab without withdrawal of capital."
People who do things as K. K. outlined often find that the
appreciation in value does make up—and sometimes it exceeds
—capital withdrawals. But nothing guarantees this will happen, and if you plump cash down for a withdrawal plan, you
should be aware of the risk which Fred pointed out.

A withdrawal setup is applicable to things other than mutual
funds. Some people practice it with stocks, particularly professional investors who live on the increase of their corporate
flocks and herds.

"Trying for ordinary dividends can be an illusion," one such
investor told me. "If I have to invest to get high dividends, on
retirement or at any other time, I have warped my investment
judgment by this income bias. I'm not selecting the best stocks
for a day of fast inflation. Instead, at the beginning of a year I
decide how much cash I want every month. Then each quarter, cash is withdrawn from the investment pool of capital. By
doing this and forgetting dividends, I can make the capital
which I have depleted by, say 10 percent, increase by 20 percent, even 30 or 40 percent."

This, too, is a risky way of doing things, although for people
who know their Wall Street methodology, it is often highly
effective and provides for both living expenses during retirement and a fling at further inflation hedging.

A withdrawal plan is not limited to stocks and mutual funds.
If you own property, you can sell bits and chunks. You can
liquidate some participations. But you should always have in
mind the reality that you are depleting capital. Risks are
greater than in working with the liquid merchandise of Wall
Street.

Go Keogh

The Keogh plan is for self-employed persons. It gives to professional and business people the tax-deferred retirement
planning which those who enjoy corporate or public pension
benefits have always had available.

Keogh retirement must usually be accomplished through
the use of insurance policies or purchase of mutual funds.

Since insurance policies, while needful for family protection, suffer from a disadvantage in inflationary times because they have fixed dollar value, retirement planners bent on beating the dollar dwindle will do best to employ mutuals. The following quotation is taken from my book, *How to Make Money with Mutual Funds:*

Who is a self-employed person? The U.S. Treasury Department in a guide entitled *Retirement Plans for Self-employed Individuals* states: "An individual who has earned income from personal services for any taxable year (or would have if there had been profits) shall be considered a self-employed person." The Treasury warns that the term "self-employed individual" does not include a person without earnings from personal services. Where capital is a material factor in producing income, says the Treasury, "earned income is only that portion of the net profits from the trade or business which constitutes a reasonable allowance as compensation for personal services actually rendered." Moreover, Uncle Sam warns that interest is not "earned" for the purpose of computing allowable contributions. But "if interest income is derived from financing activities which are an integral part of a taxpayer's business in which he also renders personal services, such interest income would enter into the computation." Those deriving income solely from investments cannot qualify. Likewise, if you are in public office, an employee of someone else, a U.S. citizen working for a foreign government, a newsboy or a sharecropper, you do not come up to the definition of self-employed for Keogh Plan purposes.

How much contribution is tax free? In most cases, $2,500 per year or 10 percent of self-employed income, whichever is less, is tax free. This can be deducted as income in the year during which it was put toward a Keogh retirement plan. When you begin to take out and use the retirement income, tax then becomes due. The advantage in such a setup is that most self-employed persons expect to be earning less after retirement than when the money is set aside. Thus, because they are likely to be in lower tax brackets, they can expect to pay smaller taxes than if the income were declarable immediately.

Who else must be included? Employees who have been with you for three years or more must be written into the plan. The

contributions you make toward their retirement are "vested"—
that is, nonforfeitable—should the employee resign or be fired.
Must contributions be the same each year? The law recognizes
two different kinds of retirement plans. One is called a pension
plan. Says the Treasury Department:

"A plan under which employer contributions are dependent
upon profits is a profit-sharing plan. Hence it would appear that
only profit-sharing plans would apply to self-employed individuals. For qualification purposes, if a contribution on behalf
of common law employees is required under the plan without
regard to profits, the plan is treated as a pension plan. On the
other hand, if contributions on behalf of all participants are
related to the profits or earned income of the employer, a plan
is considered a profit-sharing plan."

Dovetail Social Security

"Social security? That's a pension for when we grow old, isn't
it?" Alice asked as the three couples continued their discussion.

Social security is a great deal more than that. It embraces
medical help for the aged (Medicare and Medicaid), old age
and survivors insurance, and disability benefits. "I'm against
most of this," Alice said, when the scope of the program was
pointed out. "Why should I use something that I believe bad?"
"Because 'good' and 'bad' are relative terms," K. K. said. "You
can't call something all bad which has been of assistance to so
many people. I think if we chewed this over, we would discover
that your adjective 'bad' applies more to your view on how
they do certain things than to the concept of social security
itself. Besides—that isn't the point unless you aim to be as
hidebound as those old Western trail bosses sometimes manage
to be. Social security is here. It should be part of a retirement
package. With the cost of health care rising rapidly, we'll need
Medicare and Medicaid if we aren't to lose out when we move
into that bunkhouse at the trail's end."

Some of the things social security currently covers are outlined in Table 4. For full details, ask the U.S. Department
of Health, Education, and Welfare to send you *Social Security
Programs in the United States,* priced at 55 cents. Specific benefits and rules are subject to change.

The Role of Life Insurance

"Life insurance?" asked Jill incredulously. "You must be kidding. What place has that in an inflation package for retirement?"

"Plenty, my love," said her husband as he poured a fresh highball. "Another drink, anyone? If I die tomorrow, J. J., what happens to our inflation planning? Unless there is hard,

TABLE 4   *Cash Benefits Payable and Insured Status Requirements under OASDHI*

Retirement Benefits	
Monthly payments, equal to 100 percent of the primary insurance amount, are payable to:	*If the worker is:*
A retired worker 65 or over[1]	Fully insured
And monthly payments, equal to 50 percent of the primary insurance amount,[2] are payable to a worker's:	
Wife or dependent divorced wife 65 or over[3]	Fully insured
Dependent child under 18, or 18 through 21 if in school	Fully insured
Dependent son or daughter 18 or over who has been disabled since before 18	Fully insured
Wife of any age if caring for an entitled child under 18 or disabled ..	Fully insured
Dependent husband 65 or over[3]	Fully insured
Monthly payments, equal to $40, are payable at age 72 to:	
A worker who reached age 65 (62 for women) before 1957	Transitionally insured
And monthly payments, equal to $20, are payable at age 72 to a worker's:	
Wife who reached age 72 before 1969.	Transitionally insured

Survivor Benefits	
Monthly payments, equal to 82½ percent[4] of the primary insurance	

	If at death the worker is:
amount, are payable to a worker's: Widow or dependent surviving divorced wife 62 or over[5]	Fully insured
Dependent widower 62 or over[6]	Fully insured
One dependent parent 62 or over	Fully insured

Monthly payments, equal to 75 percent of the primary insurance amount, are payable to a worker's:

Widow or dependent surviving divorced wife under 62 if caring for an entitled child under 18 or disabled	Either fully or currently insured
Dependent child under 18, or 18 through 21 if in school	Either fully or currently insured
Dependent son or daughter 18 or over who has been disabled since before 18	Either fully or currently insured
Dependent parent 62 or over, when both parents are entitled	Fully insured

Lump-sum payment, equal to the lesser of three times the worker's primary insurance amount or $255, may be paid to a worker's:

Widow or widower, if living with the worker in the same household at the time of his death. Otherwise, the lump-sum can go to pay the burial expenses	Either fully or currently insured

Monthly payments, equal to $40, are payable at age 72 to a worker's:

Widow who reached age 72 before 1969	Transitionally insured

Disability Benefits

Monthly payments, equal to the amounts payable in retirement cases,[7] are payable to:

If the worker is:

A disabled worker under 65 and his dependents[8]	Fully insured and has 20 quarters of coverage in the 40 calendar quarters ending with the quarter in which he became disabled[9]

TABLE 4   (Continued)

Special Benefits

Monthly payments at age 72 are payable to:	*If the person, or couple, meet:*
A single person, equal to $40 .... A couple, equal to $60	Special requirements for insured status which apply only to this type of payment

[1] Reduced benefits are payable at age 62; benefit amount is permanently reduced by 5/9 of one percent for each month the benefit is paid before 65.

[2] Amount of wife's, divorced wife's, or dependent husband's benefit is subject to a maximum of $105 per month

[3] Reduced benefits are payable at age 62; benefit amount is permanently reduced by 25/36 of one percent for each month the benefit is paid before 65.

[4] Certain remarried widows and widowers receive 50 percent of deceased spouse's primary insurance amount, but not in excess of $105 a month.

[5] Reduced benefits are payable at age 60; benefit amount is permanently reduced by 5/9 of one percent for each month the benefit is paid before age 62. If disabled, reduced benefits are payable at age 50, ranging from 50 percent of deceased spouse's primary insurance amount for entitlement at age 50 up to 71½ percent at age 60 (the same amount payable to an aged widow at that age).

[6] If disabled, reduced benefits are payable, ranging from 50 percent of deceased spouse's primary insurance amount at age 50 up to 82½ percent at age 62 (the amount payable to an aged widower at that age).

[7] Except that benefits for a disabled worker before age 65 are not reduced unless he previously received a reduced insurance benefit.

[8] Same categories as in retirement cases.

[9] Special alternative insured status for young workers—if disabled before age 31, one-half the quarters after age 21 up to date of disability; or if disabled before age 24, one-half the quarters in the 3 years ending with the quarter of disability but not less than 6.

cold cash, even though that cash is depreciating all the time, then security is missing from the plan. We can succeed without insurance only if you believe no unexpected event can arise. Life insurance is the glue which makes the rest of the plan stick together."

FIVE QUESTIONS:

Q. *Suppose I set up a withdrawal plan. Part of retirement income is from dividends and a small portion from sale of mutual fund shares. Will I have to pay income tax on all of this?*

A. No. Your income tax would depend upon two things: how much is classed as dividend pass-along by the mutual fund (assuming that your withdrawal vehicle is a mutual) and how much is ordinary dividend from the corporation (when you use stocks). Of the portion that came from the sale of some shares, how much of the sale price (if any) represented a profit on the shares? If you have a profit on shares, determine whether it was long-term or short-term; the two kinds of profit are taxed at different rates.

Sounds complicated, but it is not. Assuming a long-term profit, you will probably be taxed at a lower rate than if the whole withdrawal were to consist of dividend with no leavening of capital gain. You might have a loss on shares sold; then you not only pay no tax on that portion, but you can use the loss to advantage on your return.

(It's wise, of course, to sell the stocks you have held longer than the minimum-tax holding period in order to obtain long-term tax treatment of profits. Stocks held for a shorter time will incur taxation as ordinary income.)

Q. *Would you advocate buying a go-go fund or performance stock, withdrawing some every year, with the aim of capital enhancement even after retirement?*

A. This is something like asking where one should use a power saw or a hammer. The answer depends upon who you are and what job you want to do. Power saws aren't good for driving nails, nor hammers for wrenching pipes.

If you have the kind of personality which, even in the calmer retirement years, wants action—maybe yes. *If* you are pretty skillful at the stock market—maybe yes. *If* you can afford the risks, bearing in mind a few of the go-go mutual funds which went-went to the extent of 50 percent losses in the 1969 bear market, and the performance stocks which were dumped by investors during that same sad year so that half their values were occasionally erased—maybe yes. *If* you have enough security over and above this go-go stake to keep you going should you prove inept in its management, should the year be a bad one and you not nimble enough to have avoided bear traps, or should other things go badly—maybe yes.

Think about all of those *ifs* before you remove the "maybe" from "maybe yes."

Q. *Under a Keogh Plan, who holds the mutual fund shares during the years while a retirement fund builds up?*

A. An "approved' 'institution. Usually, this means a bank which acts as custodian. If you opt for insurance as the vehicle for Keogh investment, no question arises. You are also allowed variable annuity insurance or a bank-administered trust plan. And, of course, mutual funds.

Q. *Will social security penalize me during retirement years if I have other sources of income?*

A. Sometimes yes, sometimes no.

Should you earn substantial sums (the dollar amount which is considered "substantial" varies and should be checked at the time), then social security payments might be restricted. Some income is exempt, however, and all restrictions end after a beneficiary reaches age 72. There are special rules for payments to beneficiaries outside the borders of the U.S.; if you intend to leave the country for thirty days or more, check with local social security people.

Q. *Explain disability payments on social security before age sixty-five.*

A. Here's a quote from a useful little booklet, *Your Social Security,* which is obtainable at the Government Printing Office, Washington, D.C. 20402, for 15 cents:

> Do not wait too long after you are disabled to apply for benefits; if you wait more than a year, you may lose benefits. Payments may begin with the 7th full month of disability.
>
> If you are found eligible for disability insurance benefits, you will remain eligible as long as you are disabled. When you reach

65, your benefit will be changed to retirement payments at the same rate.

A person is considered disabled only if he has a severe physical or mental condition which—

1. Prevents him from working, and

2. Is expected to last (or has lasted for at least 12 months) or is expected to result in death.

Index

Index

A

Accounting, 54–55, 170–171

Accumulative plans, 7, 77

Agriculture, U.S. Department of, 135, 156, 177, 192
  budgeting guides, family, 175–176, 192
  commodity market appraisals, 150
  meat standards, 176

Alaskan oil, 117–118

American Depository Receipts (ADRs), 59

Amusement areas (*see* Resort land)

Apartment buildings, 92–93

Assets in the ground, 27, 30

Assignats, 10–12, 29

Automobiles, 5, 9, 173
  leasing of, 38
  pricing variations on, 184
  saving on costs of, 184–185
  trailer stock, 51
  Volkswagens, 11, 29

B

Bank borrowing, 24

Bank loans, 34–36, 42, 45

Banks:
  central, 16–19, 24
    creation of money by, 16–21
  savings, 45

Bethlehem Steel Corporation, 28

332
Markstein, David
How you can beat inflation.

2-72